GREAT WESTERN RAILWAY
LOCOMOTIVE ALLOCATIONS
FOR 1934

REV. NIGEL J. POCOCK

AND

IAN HARRISON

WILD SWAN PUBLICATIONS LTD.

Severn Tunnel Junction shed on 30th July 1939 showing the very obvious new extension believed completed during the previous year.

W. A. Camwell

INTRODUCTION

The locomotive allocations given in this book are taken from the original Great Western Railway locomotive registers, now kept in the Public Record Office at Kew. These registers record the allocation of each engine at 1st January, together with subsequent allocations at the end of thirteen 'four week' periods through the year. However, the movement of locomotives between sheds would clearly have occurred at any time throughout each four week period, and the actual transfer dates are often noted in the 1934 register. For instance, loco No. 216 is shown as moving to Swindon F. Pool from Banbury on 6th February 1934, whilst the four week period during which this occurred did not end until 10th February. The dates at the end of each period were: 13th January, 10th February, 10th March, 7th April, 5th May, 2nd June, 30th June, 28th July, 25th August, 22nd September, 20th October, 17th November and 15th December.

This book forms a companion to the *Locomotive Allocations for 1921* (also published by Wild Swan Publications) which showed the situation just prior to the Grouping, when the many smaller railway companies in South Wales were absorbed. This volume for 1934 gives allocations from the middle of the Grouping period, and reflects a particularly interesting time, when some locomotives of the older Dean and Armstrong classes, such as the '517' and 'Barnum' classes, still remained, alongside the more modern Collett locomotives. A number of the steam railmotors were also still in service. Within a short period, many of these older types had been swept away, replaced by further 'Halls', 'Granges' and modern classes of pannier tank, etc.

The locomotive shed names in the 1934 register also show some changes from the 1921 designations. For example, Old Oak Common (or O.O.C.) was previously termed Paddington in the 1921 register. The 1934 register also distinguishes between locomotives in the works and those at the running shed for each repairing depot: Bath Road, Bristol; Barry; Ebbw Junction, Newport; Newton Abbot; Oswestry; Stafford Road, Wolverhampton; Swindon; and Tyseley, whilst the 1921 register only gives this information separately for Swindon. It has therefore been possible to give a complete list of those locomotives in the works on 1st January 1934, together with those which were stored out of use. One of the appendices also deals with those locomotives which were held at their home sheds awaiting a visit to the works.

The GWR registers record the allocation for each locomotive, but do not provide lists of engines stabled at each shed. As such information is of great interest to railway historians and modellers, the date from the register has been sorted to produce shed by shed allocations. These should be taken as a guide to typical locomotive stocks at each shed, rather than an absolute statement of the engines working from a given shed on, say, 1st January 1934. For example, it is well known that the engines working on some branch lines were regularly exchanged with similar locos from the parent shed, often on a weekly basis.

The 1934 register also gives details of the tenders paired with each tender locomotive. This information is reproduced in an appendix, and should prove invaluable for locomotive students and modellers.

The photographs have been chosen to represent the period and in many cases it has been possible to find views of locomotives at the sheds to which they were allocated on 1st January 1934. As with the companion volume, the emphasis has again been given to showing the smaller and less prestigious engines, rather than the express locos which are more often featured in publications.

Nigel Pocock and Ian Harrison

The interior of **Swindon** roundhouse in April 1932, with engines No. 2913 *Saint Andrew*, '43XX' No. 4337, and former MSWJ 4—4—0 No. 1121 in view. Another MSWJ 4—4—0 is visible to the left.

Photomatic

LOCOMOTIVE ALLOCATIONS

ALEXANDRA (NEWPORT & SOUTH WALES) DOCKS & RAILWAY

0–6–2T ANDREW BARCLAY (dia. A25)
190 Pill
191 Pill
192 Pill

0–6–0T KERR STUART (dia. B13)
666 Pill
667 Pill

0–6–0T HAWTHORN LESLIE (dia. B41)
671 Pill

0–6–0T PECKETT (dia. B1)
680 Oswestry Factory

2–6–2T HAWTHORN LESLIE (dia. W)
1205 Pill
1206 Pill

0–4–0T ALEXANDRA (dia. S)
1341 Radyr Junction

BARRY RAILWAY

0–6–2T 'B' CLASS

198	Radyr Junction	214	Radyr Junction
200	Radyr Junction	224	Barry
206	Radyr Junction	226	Radyr Junction
207	Radyr Junction	227	Radyr Junction
210	Barry	229	Barry
212	Barry	230	Radyr Junction
213	Radyr Junction	231	Barry

0–6–2T 'B1' CLASS

234	Barry	260	Barry
235	Barry	261	Barry
238	Abercynon	262	Barry
240	Radyr Junction	263	Barry
242	Barry	264	Barry
243	Barry	265	Barry
244	Barry	266	Barry
246	Radyr Junction	267	Abercynon
247	Barry Factory	268	Abercynon
248	Barry	269	Barry
250	Radyr Junction	270	Barry
252	Barry	271	Barry
253	Barry	272	Barry
254	Barry	273	Barry
256	Barry	274	Barry
257	Barry	275	Barry
258	Barry	276	Barry
259	Barry	277	Barry

0–6–0T 'F' CLASS

711	Cathays (stored)	721	Cardiff East Dock
713	Cathays (stored)	722	Cathays (stored)
714	Cathays	723	Cathays
717	Cardiff East Dock	725	Cathays
718	Cardiff East Dock	754	Cathays (stored)
719	Cathays	780	Cardiff East Dock
720	Cathays (stored)		

0–6–0T 'E' CLASS
782 Barry
783 Barry
784 Barry

BIRKENHEAD RAILWAY

0–4–0T SHARP STEWART
96 Croes Newydd

BRECON & MERTHYR RAILWAY

0–6–2T R. STEPHENSON (dia. A15)
11 Pill
21 Ebbw Junction
332 Ebbw Junction
504 Pill
698 Pill
888 Pill
1084 Pill
1113 Pill

0–6–2T R. STEPHENSON (dia. A17)

1372	Ebbw Junction	1375	Ebbw Junction
1373	Ebbw Junction	1668	Ebbw Junction
1374	Ebbw Junction	1670	Ebbw Junction

0–6–0T J. FOWLER (dia. A105)
2186 Ebbw Junction

0–6–0T SHARP STEWART (dia. A106)
2190 Didcot

BRISTOL & EXETER RAILWAY

0–6–0T BRISTOL
1376 Oswestry

BURRY PORT & GWENDRAETH VALLEY RAILWAY

0–6–0T HUDSWELL CLARKE (dia. A109)

2162	Llanelly	2167	Burry Port
2165	Burry Port	2168	Burry Port
2166	Swansea East Dock		

0–6–0T HUDSWELL CLARKE (dia. A110)
2163 Burry Port

0–6–0T AVONSIDE (dia. A112)
2176 Llanelly

0–6–0T CHAPMAN & FURNEAUX (dia. A113)
2192 Neath

0–6–0T CHAPMAN & FURNEAUX (dia. B10)
2193 Burry Port

0–6–0T AVONSIDE (dia. A114)

2194	Weymouth	2195 Weymouth

Ex-Cambrian Railways '73' Class 0–6–0 No. 875 at Aberystwyth in 1934. *L & GRP cty. David & Charles*

0–6–0T AVONSIDE (dia. A111)
2196 Danygraig

0–6–0T HUDSWELL CLARKE (dia. B11)
2197 Llanelly

0–6–0T HUDSWELL CLARKE (dia. B12)
2198 Burry Port

CAMBRIAN RAILWAYS

2–6–2T VALE OF RHEIDOL RAILWAY
   7 Aberystwyth (Narrow Gauge)
   8 Aberystwyth (Narrow Gauge)
1213 Aberystwyth (Narrow Gauge)

0–6–0T EX-LAMBOURN VALLEY RAILWAY
 819 Moat Lane

0–6–0T EX-MAWDDWY RAILWAY
 824 Oswestry

0–6–0T WELSHPOOL & LLANFAIR RAILWAY
 822 Welshpool (Narrow Gauge)
 823 Welshpool (Narrow Gauge)

0–6–0 '15' CLASS

844 Oswestry	892 Swindon Works
849 Oswestry	893 Machynlleth
855 Welshpool	894 Machynlleth
864 Portmadoc	895 Oswestry
873 Oswestry	896 Oswestry
887 Oswestry	

0–6–0 '73' CLASS

875 Aberystwyth	882 Oswestry
876 Moat Lane	884 Machynlleth
878 Oswestry	885 Moat Lane
880 Oswestry	

0–6–0 SMALL GOODS CLASS

898 Machynlleth	908 Didcot
900 Oswestry	910 Oswestry

2–4–0T SMALL SIDE TANK CLASS
1196 Oswestry
1197 Oswestry

CARDIFF RAILWAY

0–6–2T KITSON (dia. K)
 152 Treherbert

0–6–2T KITSON (dia. L/A41)
 154 Barry
 155 Cardiff East Dock

0–6–0T HUDSWELL CLARKE (dia. A74/B36)
 681 Cardiff East Dock
 682 Cardiff East Dock
 683 Cardiff East Dock
 684 Cardiff East Dock

0–4–0T KITSON (dia. O)
1338 Cathays (stored)

CLEOBURY MORTIMER & DITTON PRIORS LIGHT RAILWAY

0–6–0T MANNING WARDLE
 28 Kidderminster
 29 Kidderminster

CORNWALL MINERALS RAILWAY

0–6–0T F. TREVITHICK
1393 Danygraig
1395 Swindon
1396 Swindon
1398 Swindon
1399 Swindon

CORRIS RAILWAY (NARROW GAUGE)

0–4–2T FALCON E & C Co.
3 Corris

0–4–2T KERR STUART
4 Corris

LISKEARD & LOOE RAILWAY

2–4–0T ANDREW BARCLAY
1308 Oswestry

LLANELLY & MYNYDD MAWR RAILWAY

0–6–0T ANDREW BARCLAY (dia. B45)
312 Llanelly

0–6–0T HUDSWELL CLARKE (dia. B37)
339 Llanelly

0–6–0T HUDSWELL CLARKE (dia. B34)
359 Swansea East Dock

0–6–0T MANNING WARDLE
704 Llanelly

0–6–0T HUDSWELL CLARKE (dia. B59)
803 Danygraig

MIDLAND & SOUTH WESTERN JUNCTION RAILWAY

0–6–0 BEYER PEACOCK

1003	Gloucester	1008	Swindon
1004	Kingham	1009	Gloucester
1005	Gloucester	1010	Gloucester
1006	Gloucester	1011	Swindon
1007	Swindon	1013	Swindon

4–4–0 TYRRELL

1119	Swindon	1124	Swindon
1121	Swindon	1126	Gloucester
1122	Cheltenham High Street	1128	Cheltenham High St
1123	Cheltenham High Street		

2–4–0 DÜBS
1334 Didcot
1335 Didcot
1336 Swindon Works

PORT TALBOT RAILWAY & DOCKS

0–6–2T R. STEPHENSON (dia. A35)

184	Duffryn Yard	187	Duffryn Yard
186	Duffryn Yard	188	Duffryn Yard

0–6–0T HUDSWELL CLARKE (dia. A89)
812 Duffryn Yard
813 Duffryn Yard

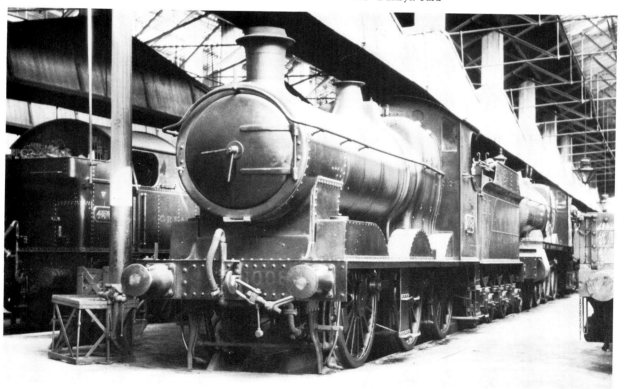

Former Midland & South Western Railway 0–6–0 No. 1008 inside the running shed at Swindon during 1933.
L & GRP, courtesy David & Charles

0—8—2T SHARP STEWART (dia. A)

1358 Duffryn Yard
1359 Duffryn Yard

POWLESLAND & MASON

0—4—0T PECKETT (dia. Y)

696 Swansea East Dock
779 Swansea East Dock
935 Swansea East Dock

0—4—0T HAWTHORN LESLIE (dia. W)

942 Swansea East Dock

RHONDDA & SWANSEA BAY RAILWAY

0—6—2T KITSON (dia. P)

164 Duffryn Yard
167 Danygraig

0—6—2T KITSON (dia. R/T)

169 Danygraig   172 Duffryn Yard
171 Duffryn Yard   173 Duffryn Yard

0—6—2T KITSON (dia. S)

177 Danygraig
178 Danygraig
179 Duffryn Yard

0—6—0T BEYER PEACOCK (dia. A88)

802 Duffryn Yard
805 Danygraig
806 Duffryn Yard

RHYMNEY RAILWAY

0—6—2T 'R' CLASS

30 Cathays   39 Rhymney
31 Cardiff East Dock 40 Cathays
32 Radyr Junction   41 Radyr Junction
34 Rhymney   42 Rhymney
35 Radyr Junction   43 Radyr Junction
36 Radyr Junction   44 Radyr Junction
37 Cardiff East Dock 46 Rhymney
38 Cathays

0—6—2T 'M' CLASS

33 Cathays   49 Radyr Junction
47 Radyr Junction   50 Radyr Junction
48 Radyr Junction   51 Cathays

0—6—2T 'A1' CLASS

52 Barry   65 Cathays (stored)
53 Cardiff East Dock 66 Barry
54 Cardiff East Dock 67 Cardiff East Dock
56 Cardiff East Dock 68 Cathays (stored)
62 Cathays (stored)   69 Cathays (stored)
63 Cathays (stored)   70 Cathays (stored)
64 Cathays (stored)   73 Cathays (stored)

0—6—2T 'A' CLASS

55 Barry   61 Cathays (stored)
57 Cardiff East Dock 71 Cathays (stored)
58 Barry   72 Cardiff East Dock
59 Barry   74 Cathays
60 Cathays (stored)   75 Cathays (stored)

0—6—2T 'P1' CLASS

76 Rhymney
77 Rhymney

0—6—2T 'AP' CLASS

78 Dowlais   80 Rhymney
79 Rhymney   81 Rhymney

0—6—2T 'P' CLASS

82 Dowlais
83 Rhymney

0—6—2T 'K' CLASS

136 Rhymney   139 Cae Harris
138 Cae Harris   141 Rhymney

0—6—0T 'S1' CLASS

604 Cardiff East Dock
605 Cardiff East Dock
606 Cardiff East Dock

0—6—0T 'S' CLASS

608 Cardiff East Dock 610 Cardiff East Dock
609 Cardiff East Dock 611 Cardiff East Dock

SOUTH DEVON RAILWAY

2—4—0T SWINDON

1300 Exeter

SWANSEA HARBOUR TRUST

0—4—0T ANDREW BARCLAY

701 Swansea East Dock

0—4—0T PECKETT (dia. Y)

929 Swansea East Dock
968 Swansea East Dock
1098 Swansea East Dock

0—4—0T HUDSWELL CLARKE (dia. X)

943 Swansea East Dock

0—4—0T HAWTHORN LESLIE (dia. Q)

974 Swansea East Dock

0—6—0T PECKETT (dia. B33)

1085 Danygraig
1086 Danygraig

TAFF VALE RAILWAY

0—6—2T 'O4' CLASS

236	Cardiff Canton	298	Coke Ovens
278	Abercynon	299	Abercynon
279	Treherbert	300	Cardiff Canton
280	Cardiff Canton	301	Ferndale
281	Cathays (stored)	302	Aberdare
282	Aberdare	310	Cardiff Canton
283	Cardiff Canton	311	Aberdare
284	Cardiff Canton	313	Cardiff Canton
285	Cathays (stored)	314	Cardiff Canton
286	Cardiff Canton	315	Cathays (stored)
287	Abercynon	317	Cardiff Canton
288	Abercynon	318	Cardiff Canton
289	Abercynon	319	Cardiff East Dock
290	Ferndale	320	Cathays
291	Cathays	321	Ferndale
292	Cathays	324	Cathays
293	Caerphilly Works	333	Cathays (stored)
294	Aberdare	409	Treherbert
295	Cardiff East Dock	414	Coke Ovens
296	Aberdare	420	Cardiff Canton
297	Cardiff East Dock		

0—6—2T 'A' CLASS

335	Pontypool Road	360	Cathays
337	Abercynon	361	Barry
343	Cathays	362	Aberdare
344	Merthyr	364	Cathays
345	Barry	365	Treherbert
346	Cathays	366	Treherbert
347	Cathays	367	Cathays
348	Cathays	368	Treherbert
349	Cardiff Canton	370	Caerphilly Works
351	Coke Ovens	371	Cathays
352	Coke Ovens	372	Barry Factory
356	Coke Ovens	373	Treherbert
357	Caerphilly Works	374	Aberdare

375	Cathays	391	Cathays
376	Cathays	393	Cathays
377	Barry	394	Barry
378	Treherbert	397	Coke Ovens
379	Barry	398	Coke Ovens
380	Coke Ovens	399	Treherbert
381	Cardiff Canton	401	Coke Ovens
382	Caerphilly Works	402	Coke Ovens
383	Cathays	403	Cathays
384	Barry	404	Barry
385	Pontypool Road	406	Cathays
386	Barry	408	Swansea East Dock
387	Barry	438	Danygraig
388	Barry	439	Barry
389	Barry	440	Barry
390	Cathays	441	Barry

0—6—2T 'O3' CLASS

410	Cardiff Canton
411	Cardiff Canton
430	Ferndale

0—6—2T 'N' CLASS

486	Treherbert

0—6—2T 'M1' CLASS

487	Cardiff Canton	577	Caerphilly Works
506	Cathays	584	Cardiff Canton
573	Coke Ovens		

0—6—0T 'H' CLASS

792	Treherbert	794	Treherbert
793	Treherbert		

WHITLAND & CARDIGAN RAILWAY

0—6—0T FOX WALKER

1331 Weymouth

Ex-Taff Vale Railway 0—6—2T of Class O4, No. 302, rests with a pannier tank in the corner of the roundhouse shed at Aberdare, during 1935.
L & GRP cty. David & Charles

0–4–0T SENTINEL SHUNTER
13   Old Oak Common

0–4–0T WOLVERHAMPTON
45   Croes Newydd

0–4–0T BEYER PEACOCK
92   Stafford Road

0–6–0 '322' BEYER GOODS
354   Leamington

0–6–0 '388' ARMSTRONG STANDARD GOODS
1094   Stourbridge
1195   Oxley

0–4–2T '517' CLASS

205	Aberayron	829	Ross
215	Goodwick	830	Newton Abbot
216	Banbury	831	Newton Abbot
217	Swindon	833	Weymouth
219	Weymouth	835	Swindon
517	Stafford Road Factory	837	Oswestry
522	Oswestry	845	Carmarthen
523	Oswestry	848	Goodwick
525	Chippenham	1154	Ebbw Junction
528	Chippenham	1155	Swindon Works
533	Kington	1157	Leamington
538	Newcastle Emlyn	1159	Didcot
542	Wallingford	1161	Llantrisant
548	Aberayron	1162	Newton Abbot
558	Neath	1163	Weymouth
559	Carmarthen	1164	Oswestry
566	Ebbw Junction	1426	Swindon
570	Reading	1427	Abingdon
571	Swindon	1430	Penmaenpool
574	Reading	1433	Swindon
828	Hereford	1436	Swindon

1438	Aylesbury	1472	St. Philip's Marsh
1440	Swindon (Tetbury)	1473	Oxford
1442	Stafford Road	1477	Swindon
1443	Ashburton	1478	Oswestry
1444	Chippenham	1482	Croes Newydd
1465	Weymouth	1485	Llantrisant
1466	Swindon Works	1486	Merthyr
1468	Goodwick	1487	Newton Abbot
1470	Merthyr	1488	Croes Newydd

2–4–0T '455' METRO TANK CLASS

457	Oxford	1500	Newton Abbot Factory
464	Worcester	3561	Gloucester
470	Newton Abbot	3562	Shrewsbury
617	Llantrisant	3563	Shrewsbury
967	Llantrisant	3564	Slough
971	Ebbw Junction	3565	Southall
975	Ebbw Junction	3566	Croes Newydd
983	Goodwick	3567	Old Oak Common
986	St. Philip's Marsh	3568	Old Oak Common
1404	Marlow	3569	Shrewsbury
1408	Llantrisant	3570	Old Oak Common
1410	Bala	3581	Truro
1415	Gloucester	3582	Swindon Stock Shed
1420	Aberdare	3583	Marlow
1445	Ebbw Junction	3584	Llantrisant
1446	St. Blazey	3585	Fairford
1454	Aberdare	3586	Old Oak Common
1455	Ross	3587	Newton Abbot Factory
1459	Gloucester	3588	Fairford
1463	Truro	3589	Oxford
1464	Truro	3590	St. Blazey
1492	Chester	3591	Old Oak Common
1493	Llantrisant	3592	Old Oak Common
1494	Swindon	3594	Cardiff Canton
1495	Merthyr	3595	Coke Ovens
1496	Helston	3596	Southall
1497	Swindon	3597	Coke Ovens
1498	St. Philip's Marsh	3598	Swindon F. Pool
1499	Truro	3599	Coke Ovens

A '517' Class 0–4–2 tank engine, No. 219, at its home shed Weymouth on 3rd June 1934.

W. Potter

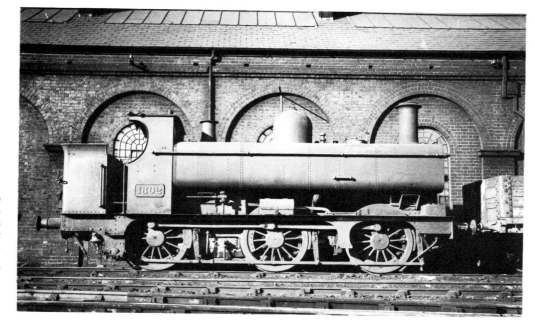

No. 1802, an 0—6—0 pannier tank of the '645' Class, stands alongside Chester locomotive shed in July 1935.

W. Potter

0—6—0T '633' CLASS

634	Old Oak Common	640	Goodwick
637	Goodwick	642	Old Oak Common
639	Goodwick	643	Old Oak Common

0—6—0T '645/1501' CLASS

646	Birkenhead	1533	Oswestry
759	Bala	1534	Pontypool Road
762	Carmarthen	1535	Aberdare
766	Chester	1536	Stafford Road
768	Wellington	1538	Gloucester
770	Pantyffynnon	1539	Croes Newydd
772	Stafford Road Factory	1540	Tyseley
1501	Tyseley	1541	Stourbridge
1502	Hereford	1542	Leamington
1505	Aberbeeg	1545	Birkenhead
1506	Stafford Road Factory	1546	Pantyffynnon
1507	Shrewsbury	1547	Stafford Road
1508	Stafford Road Factory	1548	Southall
1509	Ross	1549	Tyseley
1511	Croes Newydd	1552	Ebbw Junction
1514	Wellington	1554	Tyseley
1518	Stourbridge	1557	Severn Tunnel Junction
1519	Stafford Road Factory	1558	Stafford Road
1522	Stourbridge	1801	Aberbeeg
1523	Stourbridge	1802	Chester
1524	Wellington	1803	Stourbridge
1525	Yeovil	1806	Neath
1527	Stourbridge	1808	Birkenhead
1528	Stourbridge	1809	Stafford Road
1530	Aberdare	1810	Birkenhead
1531	Brecon	1812	Stafford Road Factory
1532	Birkenhead		

0—6—0T '655' CLASS

767	Chester	1745	Oxley
1741	Ledbury	1746	Swindon Stock Shed
1742	Tyseley	1747	Oxley
1743	Reading	1748	Stourbridge
1744	Stafford Road Factory	1749	Stafford Road

The Great Western shed at Chester is the background to this view of '655' Class 0—6—0 pannier tank No. 1773, taken in July 1935.

W. Potter

1750	Stafford Road Factory	2703	Stourbridge
1771	Stafford Road	2704	Stafford Road
1773	Chester	2705	Frome
1775	Cardiff Canton	2706	Wellington
1776	Bala	2707	Danygraig
1777	Stourbridge	2708	Stourbridge
1779	Much Wenlock	2709	Newton Abbot
1780	Trawsfynydd	2710	Stourbridge
1782	Stafford Road Factory	2711	Chester
1783	Ludlow	2712	Tyseley
1784	Stafford Road Factory	2713	Banbury
1785	Chester	2714	Tyseley
1786	Tyseley	2715	Brecon
1787	Wellington	2716	Wellington
1788	Tyseley	2717	Wellington
1789	St. Philip's Marsh	2718	Stourbridge
1790	Tyseley	2719	Stourbridge
2701	Tondu	2720	Wellington
2702	Birkenhead		

'Buffalo' Class 0—6—0 pannier tank No. 1610 stands outside Didcot shed during 1934.
Photomatic

0—6—0T '850' CLASS

850	Pill	1942	Llanelly & M. Mawr
854	Taunton	1943	Birkenhead
859	Llanelly & Mynydd Mawr	1944	St. Philip's Marsh
868	Swindon	1945	St. Philip's Marsh
869	St. Philip's Marsh	1946	Old Oak Common
870	Bridgwater	1947	Chester
872	Llanelly	1948	Llanelly
987	Swindon Works	1949	Shrewsbury
989	Danygraig	1950	Tyseley
992	Swindon (Cirencester)	1951	Stafford Road
997	Llanelly	1954	Aberystwyth
1220	Worcester	1955	Tyseley
1223	St. Blazey	1956	Taunton
1225	St. Blazey	1957	Carmarthen
1226	Pill	1958	Oxford
1227	St. Blazey	1959	Birkenhead
1902	St. Philip's Marsh	1960	Croes Newydd
1903	Old Oak Common	1961	Worcester
1904	Birkenhead	1963	Carmarthen
1905	Laira	1964	St. Philip's Marsh
1907	Burry Port	1965	Shrewsbury
1908	Swindon Works	1966	Cardiff Canton
1909	Laira	1967	St. Philip's Marsh
1910	Whitland	1968	Shrewsbury
1911	Whitland	1969	Didcot
1912	Didcot	1970	Cardiff East Dock
1915	Westbury	1971	Caerphilly Works
1917	Birkenhead	1973	Laira
1919	Hereford	1974	Llanelly & M. Mawr
1921	Swindon F. Pool	1975	Llanelly
1922	Laira	1976	Swindon Stock Shed
1923	Cardigan	1978	Burry Port
1924	Machynlleth	1979	Burry Port
1925	Taunton	1980	St. Philip's Marsh
1928	Cardiff East Dock	1982	Carmarthen
1929	Burry Port	1983	Whitland
1930	Exeter	1985	Laira
1931	Cardiff Canton	1988	Llanelly
1935	Lambourn	1989	Worcester
1936	Burry Port	1990	Cardiff Canton
1937	Burry Port	1991	Llanelly
1938	Bath Road	1992	Exeter
1941	Llanelly	1993	Taunton

1994	Whitland	2009	Pontypool Road
1996	Southall	2010	Shrewsbury
1998	Cardiff Canton	2011	Carmarthen
1999	Laira	2012	Aberystwyth
2000	Cardiff East Dock	2013	Bath Road
2001	Worcester	2014	St. Philip's Marsh
2002	Burry Port	2015	St. Philip's Marsh
2004	Shrewsbury	2016	Worcester
2005	Birkenhead	2017	St. Philip's Marsh
2006	Shrewsbury	2018	Llanelly
2007	St. Philip's Marsh	2019	Worcester
2008	Ebbw Junction	2020	Hereford

0—6—0T '1016' CLASS

1019	Ebbw Junction	1047	Stafford Road
1041	Shrewsbury	1072	Oxley
1045	Shrewsbury	1075	Shrewsbury

0—6—0T '1076' ('BUFFALO') CLASS

733	Duffryn Yard	1237	Banbury
738	Landore	1239	Bridport
743	Pontypool Road	1240	Reading
752	Llanelly	1245	Pontypool Road
753	Ebbw Junction	1246	Worcester
949	Bridgend	1247	Merthyr
963	Pontypool Road	1250	Oxford
1080	Croes Newydd	1254	Kidderminster
1134	Oxford	1256	Ebbw Junction
1136	Bala	1260	Leamington
1142	Neath	1265	Ebbw Junction
1145	Duffryn Yard	1268	Ebbw Junction
1148	Exeter	1269	Pontypool Road
1152	Southall	1271	Laira
1166	Yeovil	1272	Aberdare
1167	Plymouth	1276	Leamington
1169	Kidderminster	1278	Barry Factory
1171	Tondu	1279	Llanelly
1174	Tondu	1281	Weymouth
1179	Yeovil	1282	Newton Abbot
1180	Yeovil	1284	Ebbw Junction
1181	Ebbw Junction	1285	Cardiff Canton
1234	Cathays	1287	Pantyffynnon
1235	Landore	1289	Bridport

1292	Ebbw Junction	1611	Neath & Brecon
1296	Tondu	1615	Aberbeeg
1561	Tondu	1617	Exeter
1562	Newton Abbot Factory	1620	Yeovil
1565	Oxford	1623	Whitland
1566	Weymouth	1624	Yeovil
1567	Stafford Road	1629	Swansea East Dock
1568	Danygraig	1630	Neath & Brecon
1570	Swindon Works	1632	Stafford Road
1573	Taunton	1637	Neath
1574	Oxford	1638	Pantyffynnon
1577	Tondu	1641	Milford Haven
1580	Aberbeeg	1642	Llantrisant
1585	Cardiff Canton	1644	Westbury
1587	St. Blazey	1645	Bridgend
1593	Ebbw Junction	1646	Swindon Works
1597	Goodwick	1647	Ebbw Junction
1598	Yeovil	1649	Llantrisant
1599	Swindon F. Pool	1650	Swindon Works
1600	Pontypool Road	1658	Laira
1608	Neath & Brecon	1660	Swindon
1610	Didcot		

0–6–0T '1854' CLASS

905	Swindon Works	1759	Ebbw Junction
906	Neath	1760	Taunton
907	St. Philip's Marsh	1761	Laira
1702	Newton Abbot	1762	Llanelly
1703	St. Blazey	1763	Tyseley
1704	Duffryn Yard	1764	Swindon Stock Shed
1705	Pontypool Road	1765	Southall
1706	Leominster	1766	Stafford Road
1707	Merthyr	1767	Southall
1708	Severn Tunnel Junction	1768	Duffryn Yard
1709	Swansea East Dock	1769	Aberdare
1710	Swansea East Dock	1770	Tyseley
1712	Birkenhead	1791	Cardiff Canton
1713	Llantrisant	1792	St. Blazey
1714	Severn Tunnel Junction	1793	Swindon F. Pool
1715	Neath & Brecon	1794	Swindon Stock Shed
1716	Southall	1795	Llantrisant
1717	Exeter	1796	Ledbury
1718	Aberdare	1797	St. Blazey
1719	Landore	1798	Pantyffynnon
1720	Ebbw Junction	1799	Truro
1721	Merthyr	1800	Ebbw Junction
1722	Pontypool Road	1854	Milford Haven
1723	Ebbw Junction	1855	Llanelly
1725	Tondu	1856	Tondu
1726	Pill	1858	Llanelly
1727	Neath & Brecon	1859	Pantyffynnon
1729	Newton Abbot	1860	Yeovil
1730	Pontypool Road	1861	Danygraig
1731	Swindon	1862	Ebbw Junction Shops
1732	Duffryn Yard	1863	Stourbridge
1733	Duffryn Yard	1864	Ledbury
1734	Ebbw Junction	1866	Llanelly
1735	Ebbw Junction	1867	Neath
1736	St. Blazey	1868	Cardiff Canton
1737	Aberdare	1869	Stafford Road
1738	St. Blazey	1870	Tondu
1740	Duffryn Yard	1872	Oxford
1751	Oxford	1873	Merthyr
1752	Ebbw Junction	1875	Severn Tunnel Junction
1753	Exeter	1876	Newton Abbot
1754	Duffryn Yard	1877	Southall
1755	Laira	1878	Merthyr
1756	Duffryn Yard	1880	Reading
1758	St. Philips Marsh	1881	Swindon Works

1882	Neath & Brecon	1892	Stafford Road
1883	Danygraig	1893	Danygraig
1884	Aberbeeg	1894	Ebbw Junction Shops
1886	Tondu	1895	Newton Abbot
1887	Merthyr	1896	Ebbw Junction
1888	Branches Fork	1897	Exeter
1889	Caerphilly Works	1898	Kidderminster
1890	Barry Factory	1899	Taunton
1891	Pill	1900	St. Blazey

0–4–0T '1101' CLASS

1101	Danygraig	1104	Swansea East Dock
1102	Danygraig	1105	Danygraig
1103	Danygraig	1106	Danygraig

0–6–0T '1361' CLASS

1361	Plymouth	1364	Laira
1362	Newton Abbot	1365	Plymouth
1363	Plymouth		

0–6–0T '1661' CLASS

1685	Cardiff Canton

0–6–0T '1813' CLASS

1814	Pantyffynnon	1836	Southall
1815	Truro	1837	Landore
1816	Westbury	1838	Merthyr
1818	Pantyffynnon	1839	Aberdare
1819	St. Blazey	1840	Truro
1820	Ebbw Junction	1841	Weymouth
1823	Ebbw Junction	1844	Duffryn Yard
1824	Tyseley	1846	Ebbw Junction
1826	Carmarthen	1847	Severn Tunnel Junction
1827	Merthyr	1848	Didcot
1828	Swansea East Dock	1849	Pontypool Road
1831	Weymouth	1850	Southall
1835	St. Philip's Marsh	1853	Worcester

0–6–0T '2021' CLASS

2021	Pontypool Road	2049	Cardiff Canton
2022	Cardiff East Dock	2050	Exeter
2023	Chippenham	2051	Gloucester
2024	Lydney	2052	Tyseley
2025	Lydney	2053	Ebbw Junction
2026	Old Oak Common	2054	Oswestry
2027	Carmarthen	2055	Birkenhead
2028	Stafford Road Factory	2056	Carmarthen
2029	Hereford	2058	Cardiff Canton
2030	Stafford Road	2059	St. Philip's Marsh
2031	St. Philip's Marsh	2060	Chippenham
2032	Oswestry	2061	Stafford Road
2033	Ebbw Junction	2063	Ebbw Junction
2034	Pontypool Road	2064	Chippenham
2035	Cardiff Canton	2065	Birkenhead
2036	Tyseley	2066	Merthyr
2037	Pill	2067	Birkenhead
2038	Old Oak Common	2068	Moat Lane
2039	Lydney	2069	Slough
2040	Hereford	2070	Lydney
2041	Lydney	2071	Birkenhead
2042	Llanelly	2072	Southall
2043	Lydney	2073	Ebbw Junction
2044	Swindon	2074	Slough
2045	Didcot	2075	Oswestry
2046	Slough	2076	Croes Newydd
2047	Salisbury	2077	Pontypool Road
2048	Cardiff Canton	2078	Tyseley

A '2021' Class 0—6—0 saddle tank No. 2108 inside Stourbridge roundhouse shed on 24th April 1932. No. 2108 was still allocated to Stourbridge at the start of 1934.

W. Potter

2079 Swindon Works	2120 Birkenhead	2323 Portmadoc	2426 St. Philip's Marsh
2080 Pontypool Road	2121 Worcester	2325 Worcester	2427 Croes Newydd
2081 Watlington	2122 Ebbw Junction	2327 Brecon	2428 Lydney
2082 Llantrisant	2123 Barry Factory	2328 Worcester	2429 Oxford
2083 Llanelly	2124 Cardiff Canton	2332 Oxford	2430 Didcot
2084 Lydney	2125 Penzance	2336 Brecon	2431 Worcester
2085 Carmarthen	2126 St. Philip's Marsh	2337 Oswestry	2432 Whitland
2086 Cardiff East Dock	2127 Exeter	2339 Oswestry	2433 Cardiff Canton
2087 Slough	2129 Croes Newydd	2340 St. Philip's Marsh	2434 Pontypool Road
2088 Lydney	2130 Tondu	2341 Machynlleth	2435 Westbury
2089 Shrewsbury	2131 Gloucester	2342 Brecon	2436 Chester
2090 Birkenhead	2132 Pontypool Road	2343 Machynlleth	2437 St. Philip's Marsh
2091 Gloucester	2133 Pontypool Road	2345 Machynlleth	2438 Aberystwyth
2092 Tyseley	2134 Swansea East Dock	2346 Reading	2439 Tyseley
2093 Lydney	2135 Croes Newydd	2347 St. Philip's Marsh	2440 Carmarthen
2094 Pontypool Road	2136 Cardiff Canton	2348 Shrewsbury	2441 Bath Road
2095 Birkenhead	2137 Llanelly	2349 Lydney	2442 Shrewsbury
2096 Stafford Road Factory	2138 Hereford	2350 Worcester	2443 Old Oak Common
2097 Penzance	2139 Swansea East Dock	2351 St. Philip's Marsh	2444 Stafford Road Factory
2098 Pill	2140 Pontypool Road	2352 Machynlleth	2445 Aberystwyth
2099 Gloucester	2141 Cardiff Canton	2353 Machynlleth	2446 Landore
2100 Gloucester	2142 Cathays	2354 Oswestry	2447 Moat Lane
2101 Worcester	2143 Cardiff Canton	2356 Leamington	2449 Machynlleth
2102 Stourbridge	2144 Croes Newydd	2357 Salisbury	2450 Didcot
2103 Exeter	2145 Tyseley	2358 Reading	2451 Oxley
2104 Stourbridge	2146 Lydney	2359 Stourbridge	2452 Oxley
2105 Stourbridge	2147 Gloucester	2360 Llanelly	2454 Aberdare
2106 Stafford Road Factory	2148 Laira	2381 Bath Road	2455 Machynlleth
2107 Stourbridge	2149 Gloucester	2382 Llanelly	2456 Swindon
2108 Stourbridge	2150 Cardiff Canton	2383 Stafford Road	2457 Oswestry
2109 Stourbridge	2151 Lydney	2384 Gloucester	2458 Worcester
2110 Stourbridge	2152 Stourbridge	2385 Banbury	2459 Brecon
2111 Carmarthen	2153 Gloucester	2386 Stafford Road	2460 Shrewsbury
2112 Slough	2154 Ebbw Junction	2388 Stafford Road Factory	2461 St. Philip's Marsh
2113 Cardiff Canton	2155 Lydney	2389 Oxley	2462 Shrewsbury
2114 Swindon Works	2156 Lydney	2390 Neath	2463 Didcot
2115 Swindon Works	2157 Lydney	2392 Gloucester	2464 Chester
2116 Penzance	2158 Stourbridge	2393 Swindon Stock Shed	2465 Carmarthen
2117 Pontypool Road	2159 Pontypool Road	2394 Westbury	2466 Aberystwyth
2118 Lydney	2160 Pontypool Road	2395 Didcot	2467 St. Philip's Marsh
2119 Swindon		2396 Carmarthen	2468 Portmadoc
		2397 Didcot	2469 Stourbridge

4—4—2T '2221' CLASS

2222 Old Oak Common	2242 Reading	2398 Gloucester	2470 Cardiff Canton
2225 Didcot	2243 Reading	2399 Ebbw Junction Shops	2471 Swindon Works
2226 Old Oak Common	2246 Old Oak Common	2400 Wells	2472 St. Philip's Marsh
2235 Reading	2250 Old Oak Common	2401 Moat Lane	2473 St. Philip's Marsh
2239 Old Oak Common		2402 Gloucester	2474 Carmarthen
		2403 Swindon Works	2475 Shrewsbury
		2404 Reading	2476 Whitland

0—6—0 '2251' CLASS

2251 Swindon F. Pool	2261 Taunton	2405 Builth Wells	2477 Shrewsbury
2252 St. Philip's Marsh	2262 Tyseley Shops	2406 Oxley	2478 Cardiff Canton
2253 Reading	2263 Worcester	2407 Carmarthen	2479 Hereford
2254 Didcot	2264 Reading	2408 Oxley	2480 Severn Tunnel Junction
2255 Swindon Works	2265 Taunton	2409 Whitland	2481 Worcester
2256 Stafford Road Factory	2266 Taunton	2410 Taunton	2482 Taunton
2257 Stafford Road Factory	2267 Taunton	2411 Neath	2483 Llanidloes
2258 Gloucester	2268 St. Philip's Marsh	2412 Brecon	2484 Aberdare
2259 Didcot	2269 St. Philip's Marsh	2413 Stafford Road	2485 Worcester
2260 St. Philip's Marsh	2270 Chester	2414 Stafford Road	2486 Swindon F. Pool
		2415 Chippenham	2487 Carmarthen
		2416 Taunton	2488 Stafford Road

0—6—0 '2301' DEAN GOODS

2301 Swindon Works	2315 Pwllheli	2417 Llanidloes	2489 Southall
2303 Old Oak Common	2316 Moat Lane	2418 Carmarthen	2490 Machynlleth
2305 Reading	2317 St. Philip's Marsh	2419 Shrewsbury	2511 Chester
2310 Worcester	2320 Stourbridge	2421 Aberystwyth	2512 Swindon Works
2311 St. Philip's Marsh	2321 Aberystwyth	2422 Carmarthen	2513 Oxley
2313 Machynlleth	2322 Shrewsbury	2423 Stafford Road	2514 Llanidloes
		2424 Aberystwyth	2515 Worcester
		2425 Shrewsbury	2516 Brecon

'Aberdare' Class 2—6—0 No. 2623 at Chester during 1933. *Photomatic*

2517	Taunton	2549	Didcot
2518	Westbury	2550	Stafford Road Factory
2519	Hereford	2551	Worcester
2520	Portmadoc	2552	St. Philip's Marsh
2521	Severn Tunnel Junction	2553	Pwllheli
2522	Llanidloes	2554	Chester
2523	Oswestry Factory	2555	Croes Newydd
2524	Cardiff Canton	2556	Oswestry
2525	Stafford Road Factory	2557	Worcester
2526	Bath Road	2558	Llandovery
2527	Taunton	2559	Brecon
2528	Swindon	2560	Pwllheli
2529	Westbury	2561	Reading
2530	Neath	2562	Severn Tunnel Junction
2531	Banbury	2564	Swindon
2532	Didcot	2565	Whitchurch
2533	Newbury	2566	Westbury
2534	Swindon	2567	St. Philip's Marsh
2535	St. Philip's Marsh	2568	Worcester
2536	Evesham	2569	Stourbridge
2537	Weston-Super-Mare	2570	Reading
2538	Stourbridge	2571	Ebbw Junction
2539	Banbury	2572	Carmarthen
2540	Ebbw Junction	2573	Pontypool Road
2541	Swindon F. Pool	2574	Oswestry
2543	Bath Road Shops	2575	Tyseley
2544	Whitland	2576	Portmadoc
2545	Oswestry	2577	Worcester
2546	Ebbw Junction	2578	Swindon Works
2547	Winchester	2579	Chester
2548	Cardiff Canton	2580	Carmarthen

0—6—0 '2361' CLASS

2362	Old Oak Common	2373	St. Philip's Marsh
2364	Westbury	2375	Honeybourne
2368	Banbury	2376	Southall
2369	Reading	2378	Stourbridge
2370	Old Oak Common	2380	Worcester
2372	Llanelly		

2—6—0 2600 'ABERDARE' CLASS

2600	Llanelly	2641	Oxley
2601	Ebbw Junction	2642	Croes Newydd
2602	Laira	2643	Landore
2603	Severn Tunnel Junction	2644	Severn Tunnel Junction
2604	Stourbridge	2645	Llanelly
2605	Gloucester	2646	Cardiff Canton
2606	Banbury	2647	Exeter
2607	Banbury	2648	Laira
2608	Pontypool Road	2649	Pontypool Road
2609	Oxford	2650	Chester
2610	Banbury	2651	Ebbw Junction
2611	Old Oak Common	2652	Swansea East Dock
2612	Cardiff Canton	2653	Cardiff Canton
2613	Worcester	2654	Cardiff Canton
2614	Severn Tunnel Junction	2655	Stourbridge
2615	Stourbridge	2656	Pontypool Road
2616	Pontypool Road	2657	Llanelly
2617	Croes Newydd	2658	Chester
2618	Neyland	2659	Severn Tunnel Junction
2619	Cheltenham High Street	2660	Laira
2620	Swindon	2661	Hereford
2621	Stourbridge	2662	Swindon Works
2622	Oxley	2663	Swansea East Dock
2623	Chester	2664	Severn Tunnel Junction
2624	Severn Tunnel Junction	2665	Chester
2625	Llanelly	2666	Swansea East Dock
2626	Swindon Works	2667	Aberdare
2627	Gloucester	2668	Old Oak Common
2628	Llanelly	2669	Severn Tunnel Junction
2629	Swindon Works	2670	Gloucester
2630	Duffryn Yard	2671	Cardiff Canton
2631	Llanelly	2672	Cardiff Canton
2632	St. Philip's Marsh	2673	Banbury
2633	Oxley	2674	Chester
2634	Swindon F. Pool	2675	St. Philip's Marsh
2635	Cardiff Canton	2676	Exeter
2636	Swindon Works	2677	Swindon
2637	Pontypool Road	2678	St. Philip's Marsh
2638	Duffryn Yard	2679	Croes Newydd
2639	Westbury	2680	Gloucester
2640	Carmarthen		

0—6—0T '2721' CLASS

2700	Neath	2760	Merthyr
2721	Llanelly	2761	Tondu
2722	Duffryn Yard	2762	Cardiff Canton
2723	Pontypool Road	2763	Neath
2724	Ebbw Junction	2764	Ebbw Junction
2725	Truro	2765	Southall
2726	Cardiff Canton	2766	Merthyr
2727	Tondu	2767	Cardiff Canton
2728	Pill	2768	Gloucester
2729	Tondu	2769	Aberbeeg
2730	Pantyffynnon	2770	Llantrisant
2731	Pill	2771	Swindon Works
2732	Merthyr	2772	Swindon F. Pool
2733	Oxley	2773	Llantrisant
2734	Ebbw Junction	2774	Swindon Works
2735	Tondu	2775	Neath
2736	Aberbeeg	2776	Truro
2737	Newton Abbot	2777	Chester
2738	Barry Factory	2778	Oxley
2739	Aberdare	2779	Westbury
2740	St. Blazey	2780	Westbury
2741	Duffryn Yard	2781	Merthyr
2742	Aberdare	2782	Pantyffynnon
2743	Worcester	2783	Worcester
2744	Tyseley	2784	Reading
2745	Tondu	2785	St. Blazey
2746	Duffryn Yard	2786	St. Philip's Marsh
2747	Reading	2787	Southall
2748	Swindon Works	2788	Pontypool Road
2749	Pill	2789	Swansea East Dock
2750	Merthyr	2790	Pantyffynnon
2751	Duffryn Yard	2791	Stourbridge
2752	St. Blazey	2792	Duffryn Yard
2753	Tyseley	2793	Aberdare
2754	Pill	2794	Ebbw Junction
2755	St. Blazey	2795	Ebbw Junction
2756	Neath & Brecon	2796	Neath & Brecon
2757	Worcester	2797	Neath
2758	Stourbridge	2798	Pantyffynnon
2759	Llantrisant	2799	Frome

2—8—0 '2800' CLASS

2800	Llanelly	2825	Llanelly
2801	Old Oak Common	2826	Severn Tunnel Junction
2802	Severn Tunnel Junction	2827	Swindon
2803	Swindon	2828	Pontypool Road
2804	Aberdare	2829	Pontypool Road
2805	Old Oak Common	2830	Pontypool Road
2806	Neath	2831	Severn Tunnel Junction
2807	Llanelly	2832	Aberdare
2808	Aberdare	2833	Swindon Works
2809	Aberdare	2834	St. Philip's Marsh
2810	Aberdare	2835	Severn Tunnel Junction
2811	Ebbw Junction	2836	Salisbury
2812	Laira	2837	Tyseley
2813	Aberdare	2838	Pontypool Road
2814	St. Philip's Marsh	2839	St. Philip's Marsh
2815	Tyseley	2840	Swindon Works
2816	Old Oak Common	2841	Pontypool Road
2817	Banbury	2842	Landore
2818	Oxley	2843	Southall
2819	Laira	2844	Pantyffynnon
2820	Salisbury	2845	St. Philip's Marsh
2821	Aberdare	2846	Laira
2822	Severn Tunnel Junction	2847	Old Oak Common
2823	Severn Tunnel Junction	2848	St. Philip's Marsh
2824	Severn Tunnel Junction	2849	Aberdare

2850	Pontypool Road	2867	Old Oak Common
2851	Swindon	2868	Reading
2852	Severn Tunnel Junction	2869	Aberdare
2853	Severn Tunnel Junction	2870	Salisbury
2854	Southall	2871	Laira
2855	Old Oak Common	2872	Banbury
2856	Old Oak Common	2873	Swindon F. Pool
2857	Aberdare	2874	Tyseley
2858	Llanelly	2875	Tyseley
2859	Reading	2876	Severn Tunnel Junction
2860	Landore	2877	Llanelly
2861	Swindon Works	2878	Tyseley
2862	Aberdare	2879	Old Oak Common
2863	Oxford	2880	Aberdare
2864	Newton Abbot	2881	Newton Abbot
2865	Old Oak Common	2882	Neath
2866	Aberdare	2883	Swindon F. Pool

4—6—0 '2900' SAINT CLASS

2902	Ebbw Junction	2940	Bath Road
2903	Swindon	2941	Swindon Works
2905	Pontypool Road	2942	Swindon
2906	Swindon	2943	Swindon
2908	Bath Road	2944	Gloucester
2911	Taunton	2945	Stafford Road
2912	Taunton	2946	Swindon
2913	Swindon	2947	Pontypool Road
2914	Stafford Road	2948	Ebbw Junction
2915	Weston-Super-Mare	2949	Bath Road
2916	Chester	2950	Chester
2917	Cardiff Canton	2951	Gloucester
2918	Leamington	2952	Swindon Works
2920	Taunton	2953	Swindon F. Pool
2921	Gloucester	2954	Swindon
2922	Cardiff Canton	2955	Swindon
2923	Bath Road	2971	Bath Road
2924	Stafford Road	2972	Cardiff Canton
2926	Tyseley	2975	Cardiff Canton
2927	Tyseley	2976	Swindon F. Pool
2928	Shrewsbury	2977	Westbury
2929	Stafford Road	2978	Hereford
2930	Tyseley	2979	Swindon F. Pool
2931	Hereford	2980	Gloucester
2932	Swindon	2981	Swindon
2933	Westbury	2982	Ebbw Junction
2934	Taunton	2983	Cardiff Canton
2935	Swindon	2987	Taunton
2936	Chester	2988	Cardiff Canton
2937	Reading	2989	Swindon Stock Shed
2938	Swindon	2990	Cardiff Canton
2939	Swindon		

2—8—0 Ex-R.O.D. CLASS

3000	Neath	3015	Llanelly
3001	Tyseley Shops	3016	Severn Tunnel Junction
3002	Cardiff Canton	3017	Swindon
3003	Landore	3018	Pontypool Road
3004	Llanelly	3019	Swindon
3005	Reading	3020	Reading
3006	Neath	3021	Stafford Road
3007	Swindon Works	3022	Swindon Stock Shed
3008	Shrewsbury	3023	Pontypool Road
3009	Llanelly	3024	Oxley
3010	Neath	3025	Reading
3011	Neyland	3026	Reading
3012	Severn Tunnel Junction	3027	Worcester
3013	Severn Tunnel Junction	3028	Llanelly
3014	Swindon Works	3029	Gloucester

ROD Class 2–8–0 No. 3035 stands outside its home shed, St. Philip's Marsh, Bristol, during 1934. The shed itself can be seen behind the locomotive, whilst on the right is the coaling stage embankment. *L & GRP, courtesy David & Charles*

3030	Oxley	3040	Oxley
3031	Exeter	3041	Cardiff Canton
3032	Newton Abbot	3042	Carmarthen
3033	Oxley	3043	Ebbw Junction Shops
3034	Llanelly	3044	Carmarthen
3035	St. Philip's Marsh	3045	St. Philip's Marsh
3036	Aberdare	3046	Swindon
3037	Pontypool Road	3047	Old Oak Common
3038	Pontypool Road	3048	Gloucester
3039	Newton Abbot	3049	Laira

2–6–2T '3150' CLASS

3150	Banbury	3171	Brimscombe
3151	Newton Abbot	3172	Severn Tunnel Junction
3152	Newton Abbot	3173	Gloucester
3153	Newton Abbot	3174	Severn Tunnel Junction
3154	Severn Tunnel Junction	3175	Severn Tunnel Junction
3155	Newton Abbot	3176	Severn Tunnel Junction
3156	Cardiff Canton	3177	Severn Tunnel Junction
3157	Severn Tunnel Junction	3178	Severn Tunnel Junction
3158	Tyseley	3179	Severn Tunnel Junction
3159	Severn Tunnel Junction	3180	Laira
3160	Laira	3181	Laira
3161	Ebbw Junction	3182	Severn Tunnel Junction
3162	Ebbw Junction	3183	Newton Abbot
3163	Leamington	3184	Newton Abbot
3164	Gloucester	3185	Cardiff Canton
3165	Severn Tunnel Junction	3186	Taunton
3166	Newton Abbot	3187	Taunton
3167	Severn Tunnel Junction	3188	Severn Tunnel Junction
3168	Cardiff Canton	3189	Severn Tunnel Junction
3169	Severn Tunnel Junction	3190	Tyseley
3170	Ebbw Junction		

2–4–0 '3206' BARNUM CLASS

3206	Machynlleth	3217	Portmadoc
3210	Wellington	3219	Croes Newydd
3211	Croes Newydd	3222	Wellington
3213	Machynlleth	3223	Swindon Works
3216	Wellington	3225	Machynlleth

4–4–0 '3252' DUKE CLASS

3252	Stafford Road Factory	3272	Aberystwyth
3253	Oswestry	3273	Shrewsbury
3254	Oswestry	3274	Tyseley
3255	Aberystwyth	3275	Aberystwyth
3256	Didcot	3276	Stafford Road
3257	Machynlleth	3277	Stafford Road Factory
3258	Oswestry	3278	Andover Junction
3259	Swindon Works	3279	Didcot
3260	Gloucester	3280	Didcot
3261	Gloucester	3281	Stratford
3262	Aberystwyth	3282	Didcot
3263	Oswestry	3283	Westbury
3264	Aberystwyth	3284	Oswestry
3265	Oswestry	3285	Gloucester
3266	Swindon Works	3286	Reading
3267	Didcot	3287	Machynlleth
3268	Cheltenham High Street	3288	Aberystwyth
3269	Oswestry	3289	Andover Junction
3270	Machynlleth	3290	Didcot
3271	Aberystwyth	3291	Swindon F. Pool

4–4–0 '3300' BULLDOG CLASS

3300	Bath Road	3328	Hereford
3304	Reading	3330	Weymouth
3305	Bath Road	3331	Taunton
3306	Salisbury	3335	Weston-Super-Mare
3307	Hereford	3336	Exeter
3308	Hereford	3337	Hereford
3309	Wellington	3339	Pontypool Road
3313	Newton Abbot	3340	Swindon
3314	Gloucester	3341	Reading
3316	Westbury	3342	Laira
3318	Hereford	3343	Westbury
3321	Stourbridge	3344	Carmarthen
3322	Gloucester	3345	Weymouth
3323	Reading	3347	Tondu
3324	Didcot	3348	Worcester
3325	Oxford	3349	Hereford
3327	Chester	3350	Hereford

'Barnum' Class 2—4—0, No. 3217, of Portmadoc shed, eases onto the turntable at Machynlleth during 1934. In the background is ex-Cambrian Railways 0—6—0 No. 898.   *L & GRP, courtesy David & Charles*

Didcot engine No. 3280, a 'Duke' Class 4—4—0, is seen there during 1934.   *Photomatic*

Curve-framed 'Bull-dog' Class 4—4—0 No. 3323 *Etona* is seen near the water tanks at its home shed, Reading, during 1933.

Photomatic

3353 Worcester	3398 Laira	3442 Chester	3449 Worcester
3354 Westbury	3399 Banbury	3443 Newton Abbot	3450 Tyseley
3355 Hereford	3400 Neyland	3444 Barnstaple	3451 Gloucester
3356 Reading	3401 Laira	3445 Banbury	3452 Bath Road
3357 Newton Abbot	3402 Hereford	3446 Bath Road	3453 Taunton
3358 Stafford Road	3403 Tyseley	3447 Neyland	3454 Didcot
3359 Chester	3404 Reading	3448 Didcot	3455 Carmarthen
3360 Tyseley	3405 Crewe		
3361 Didcot	3406 Worcester		
3362 Swindon F. Pool	3407 Cardiff Canton	**4—4—0 '3521' CLASS**	
3363 Swindon F. Pool	3408 Southall	3557 Kidderminster	
3364 Swindon	3409 Hereford		
3366 Swindon Works	3410 Swindon Works		
3367 Bath Road	3411 Cardiff Canton	**0—4—2T '3571' CLASS**	
3368 Worcester	3412 Swindon F. Pool	3571 Stafford Road	3577 Birkenhead
3369 Tyseley	3413 St. Philip's Marsh	3573 Caerphilly Works	3578 Birkenhead
3370 Banbury	3414 Shrewsbury	3574 Leominster	3579 Birkenhead
3371 Worcester	3415 Carmarthen	3575 Birkenhead	3580 Birkenhead
3372 Hereford	3416 Barnstaple		
3373 Shrewsbury	3417 Tyseley		
3374 Shrewsbury	3418 Worcester	**2—4—2T '3600' CLASS**	
3375 Swindon	3419 Cardiff Canton	3604 Chester	3627 Birkenhead
3376 Bath Road	3420 Gloucester	3610 Old Oak Common	3628 Leamington
3377 Reading	3421 Westbury	3618 Chester	
3378 Bath Road	3422 Cardiff Canton		
3379 Bath Road	3423 Stratford		
3380 Didcot	3424 Laira	**2—6—2T '3901' CLASS**	
3381 Stafford Road	3425 Carmarthen	3901 Neath	3916 Landore
3382 Reading	3426 Stratford	3907 Landore	3919 Slough
3383 Shrewsbury	3427 Hereford		
3384 Westbury	3428 Worcester	**4—6—0 '4000' STAR CLASS**	
3385 Didcot	3429 Oxford	4001 Swindon F. Pool	4021 Shrewsbury
3386 Cardiff Canton	3430 Bath Road	4003 Old Oak Common	4022 Swindon
3387 Banbury	3431 Salisbury	4004 Landore	4023 Bath Road
3388 Hereford	3432 Weymouth	4005 Old Oak Common	4024 Exeter
3389 Westbury	3433 Bath Road	4007 Exeter	4025 Shrewsbury
3390 Carmarthen	3434 Reading	4008 Old Oak Common	4026 Exeter
3391 Salisbury	3435 Neyland	4010 Bath Road	4027 Landore
3392 Cardiff Canton	3436 Hereford	4012 Bath Road	4028 Bath Road
3393 Laira	3437 Neyland	4013 Worcester	4029 Stafford Road
3394 Worcester	3438 Swindon Works	4014 Swindon Works	4030 Landore
3395 Banbury	3439 Severn Tunnel Junction	4015 Old Oak Common	4031 Shrewsbury
3396 Bath Road	3440 Gloucester	4017 Landore	4033 Worcester
3397 Neyland	3441 Reading	4018 Landore	4034 Stafford Road
		4019 Landore	4035 Bath Road
		4020 Old Oak Common	4036 Old Oak Common

The '3571' Class 0—4—2 tanks were allocated in the north west of the Great Western system for many years. No. 3575 was a Birkenhead engine at the start of 1934, and is seen here on the turntable during July 1937.   *W. Potter*

Queen Elizabeth, No. 4036, of the 'Star' Class, at Old Oak Common on 25th May 1935; this was also her home shed at the start of 1934.
                    LCGB/Ken Nunn Collection

4038	Worcester	4056	Exeter
4039	Bath Road	4057	Landore
4040	Landore	4058	Shrewsbury
4041	Shrewsbury	4059	Landore
4042	Landore	4060	Swindon Stock Shed
4043	Bath Road	4061	Bath Road
4044	Swindon F. Pool	4062	Stafford Road
4045	Exeter	4063	Swindon Works
4046	Shrewsbury	4064	Shrewsbury
4047	Landore	4065	Stafford Road
4048	Swindon Works	4066	Stafford Road
4049	Worcester	4067	Worcester
4050	Old Oak Common	4068	Shrewsbury
4051	Shrewsbury	4069	Swindon F. Pool
4052	Old Oak Common	4070	Landore
4053	Bath Road	4071	Old Oak Common
4054	Exeter	4072	Swindon Works
4055	St. Philip's Marsh		

4—6—0 '4073' CASTLE CLASS

111	Old Oak Common	4095	Swindon Works
4000	Old Oak Common	4096	Stafford Road
4009	Cardiff Canton	4097	Stafford Road
4016	Bath Road	4098	Old Oak Common
4032	Laira	4099	Cardiff Canton
4037	Carmarthen	5000	Laira
4073	Old Oak Common	5001	Old Oak Common
4074	Landore	5002	Swindon Works
4075	Old Oak Common	5003	Old Oak Common
4076	Bath Road	5004	Cardiff Canton
4077	Laira	5005	Swindon Stock Shed
4078	Old Oak Common	5006	Laira
4079	Swindon Works	5007	Old Oak Common
4080	Laira	5008	Old Oak Common
4081	Cardiff Canton	5009	Laira
4082	Old Oak Common	5010	Newton Abbot
4083	Old Oak Common	5011	Newton Abbot
4084	Cardiff Canton	5012	Cardiff Canton
4085	Carmarthen	5013	Laira
4086	Swindon Works	5014	Newton Abbot
4087	Old Oak Common	5015	Old Oak Common
4088	Newton Abbot	5016	Newton Abbot
4089	Stafford Road	5017	Old Oak Common
4090	Swindon Works	5018	Old Oak Common
4091	Newton Abbot	5019	Newton Abbot
4092	Swindon Works	5020	Laira
4093	Cardiff Canton	5021	Laira
4094	Laira	5022	Swindon Works

2—8—0T '4200' CLASS

4200	St. Philip's Marsh	4217	Caerphilly (stored)
4201	Pill	4218	Caerphilly (stored)
4202	Caerphilly (stored)	4219	Neath
4203	Ebbw Junction	4220	Ebbw Junction
4204	Llanelly	4221	Swindon Stock Shed
4205	Ebbw Junction	4222	Caerphilly (stored)
4206	Ebbw Junction	4223	Landore
4207	Danygraig	4224	Ebbw Junction
4208	Caerphilly Works	4225	Pill
4209	Swansea East Dock	4226	Ebbw Junction
4210	Swansea East Dock	4227	Tondu
4211	Pill	4228	Aberdare
4212	Llanelly	4229	Pill
4213	Llanelly	4230	Swindon Works
4214	Caerphilly (stored)	4231	Barry
4215	St. Blazey	4232	Tondu
4216	Ebbw Junction	4233	Aberbeeg

4234	Ebbw Junction	5202	Tondu
4235	Ebbw Junction	5203	Barry
4236	Pill	5204	Aberdare
4237	Caerphilly (stored)	5205	Cardiff Canton
4238	Pill	5206	Ebbw Junction
4239	Cardiff Canton	5207	Barry
4240	Barry	5208	Barry
4241	Cardiff Canton	5209	Landore
4242	Cardiff Canton	5210	Duffryn Yard
4243	Aberbeeg	5211	Caerphilly Works
4244	Swindon Works	5212	Pantyffynnon
4245	Caerphilly (stored)	5213	Llanelly
4246	Duffryn Yard	5214	Swansea East Dock
4247	Ebbw Junction	5215	Neath
4248	Swindon Stock Shed (stored)	5216	Glyn Neath
4249	Caerphilly Works	5217	Danygraig
4250	Swansea East Dock	5218	Ebbw Junction
4251	Barry	5219	Pantyffynnon
4252	Swindon Works	5220	Pantyffynnon
4253	Ebbw Junction	5221	Swansea East Dock
4254	Glyn Neath	5222	Ebbw Junction
4255	Swansea East Dock	5223	Caerphilly (stored)
4256	Danygraig	5224	Barry
4257	Llantrisant	5225	Barry
4258	Cardiff Canton	5226	Pantyffynnon
4259	Neath	5227	Swindon Stock Shed (stored)
4260	Pontypool Road	5228	Pantyffynnon
4261	Aberdare	5229	Swansea East Dock
4262	Tondu	5230	Landore
4263	Swindon Works	5231	Swansea East Dock
4264	Pontypool Road	5232	Swansea East Dock
4265	Neath	5233	Aberdare
4266	Llantrisant	5234	Ebbw Junction
4267	Caerphilly (stored)	5235	Swansea East Dock
4268	Pill	5236	Ebbw Junction
4269	Ebbw Junction	5237	Duffryn Yard
4270	Ebbw Junction	5238	Ebbw Junction
4271	Ebbw Junction	5239	Neath
4272	Swansea East Dock	5240	Ebbw Junction
4273	Pill	5241	Ebbw Junction
4274	Duffryn Yard	5242	Swindon Stock Shed (stored)
4275	Pill	5243	Ebbw Junction
4276	Ebbw Junction	5244	Barry
4277	Llanelly	5245	Ebbw Junction
4278	Cardiff Canton	5246	Landore
4279	Ebbw Junction	5247	Pantyffynnon
4280	Caerphilly Works	5248	Ebbw Junction
4281	Llanelly	5249	Ebbw Junction
4282	Landore	5250	Landore
4283	Danygraig	5251	Barry
4284	Ebbw Junction	5252	Ebbw Junction
4285	Aberdare	5253	Swansea East Dock
4286	Ebbw Junction	5254	Glyn Neath
4287	Llantrisant	5255	Aberdare
4288	Llantrisant	5256	Caerphilly Works
4289	Ebbw Junction	5257	Cardiff Canton
4290	Aberbeeg	5258	Duffryn Yard
4291	Ebbw Junction	5259	Ebbw Junction
4292	Llanelly	5260	Ebbw Junction
4293	Caerphilly (stored)	5261	Ebbw Junction
4294	Aberdare	5262	Swansea East Dock
4295	Caerphilly (stored)	5263	Llanelly
4296	Llanelly	5264	Swindon Stock Shed (stored)
4297	Aberdare	5265	Llanelly
4298	Swindon Stock Shed	5266	Pill
4299	Pill	5267	Ebbw Junction
5200	Ebbw Junction		
5201	Barry		

Churchward Mogul No. 7311 is seen taking water alongside Chester shed in July 1935, in the company of a pannier tank and 2251 class 0—6—0.

W. Potter

5268	Neath	5281	Ebbw Junction*
5269	Swansea East Dock	5282	Ebbw Junction*
5270	Caerphilly Works	5283	Caerphilly*
5271	Aberdare	5284	Caerphilly*
5272	Swansea East Dock	5285	Ebbw Junction*
5273	Caerphilly Works	5286	Caerphilly*
5274	Duffryn Yard	5287	Swindon Stock Shed*
5275	Swindon Stock Shed*	5288	Swindon Stock Shed*
5276	Swindon Stock Shed*	5289	Swindon Stock Shed*
5277	Swindon Stock Shed*	5290	Caerphilly*
5278	Swindon Stock Shed*	5291	Ebbw Junction*
5279	Swindon Stock Shed*	5292	Swindon Stock Shed*
5280	Caerphilly*	5293	Caerphilly*
		5294	Swindon Stock Shed*

2—6—0 '4300' CLASS

4300	Aberdare	4325	Pontypool Road
4301	Ebbw Junction	4326	Westbury
4302	Pontypool Road	4327	Worcester
4303	Pontypool Road	4328	Swindon Works
4304	Taunton	4329	Tyseley
4305	Worcester	4330	Chester
4306	Gloucester	4331	Neyland
4307	Tyseley	4332	Shrewsbury
4308	Worcester	4333	Tyseley
4309	St. Philip's Marsh	4334	Ebbw Junction
4310	St. Philip's Marsh	4335	Pontypool Road
4311	Neyland	4336	Tyseley
4312	Worcester	4337	Oxley
4313	Taunton	4338	Stafford Road
4314	Westbury	4339	Chester
4315	Westbury	4340	Neyland
4316	Oxley	4341	Old Oak Common
4317	Birkenhead	4342	Oxley
4318	Ebbw Junction	4343	Tyseley
4319	Cardiff Canton	4344	Cardiff Canton
4320	Basingstoke	4345	Old Oak Common
4321	Taunton	4346	Chester
4322	Landore	4347	Croes Newydd
4323	Chester	4348	St. Philip's Marsh
4324	Banbury	4349	Westbury

4350	Swindon Works	4391	Barnstaple
4351	Birkenhead	4392	Reading
4352	Neyland	4393	Stafford Road
4353	Oxley	4394	Neath
4354	St. Philip's Marsh	4395	Oxley
4355	Severn Tunnel Junction	4396	Oxley
4356	Neyland	4397	Pontypool Road
4357	Oxley	4398	Swindon Works
4358	Oxley	4399	Neyland
4359	Worcester	5303	Worcester
4360	Cardiff Canton	5306	Severn Tunnel Junction
4361	Banbury	5310	Ebbw Junction
4362	Shrewsbury	5311	Banbury
4363	Old Oak Common	5312	Stafford Road
4364	Swindon F. Pool	5316	Pontypool Road
4365	Westbury	5317	Swindon Stock Shed
4366	Neath	5319	Swindon Works
4367	Cardiff Canton	5321	Tyseley
4368	Westbury	5323	Stafford Road
4369	Bath Road	5324	Banbury
4370	Weymouth	5330	Stafford Road
4371	Pontypool Road	5336	Ebbw Junction
4372	Ebbw Junction	5339	Reading
4373	Stafford Road	5345	Chester
4374	St. Philip's Marsh	5346	Birkenhead
4375	Tyseley	5347	Neyland
4376	Chester	5348	Chester
4377	St. Philip's Marsh	5349	Chester
4378	Cardiff Canton	5355	Swindon
4379	St. Philip's Marsh	5356	Swindon
4380	St. Philip's Marsh	5367	Weymouth
4381	Swindon Works	5370	Oxley
4382	Neyland	5371	Llanelly
4383	Swindon Works	5375	Worcester
4384	Reading	5377	Stafford Road
4385	Oxley	5380	Old Oak Common
4386	Tyseley	5385	Hereford
4387	St. Philip's Marsh	5392	Oxley
4388	Pontypool Road	5394	Gloucester
4389	Oxley	5395	Goodwick
4390	Oxley	5396	Swindon Works

* Stored

5397	Shrewsbury	6365	Carmarthen
5398	Ebbw Junction	6366	Oxley
5399	Oxley	6367	Llanelly
6300	Birkenhead	6368	Tyseley
6301	Landore	6369	Banbury
6302	Landore	6370	Worcester
6303	Bath Road	6371	Cheltenham High Street
6304	Goodwick	6372	Tyseley
6305	Bath Road	6373	Reading
6306	St. Philip's Marsh	6374	Oxley
6307	Weymouth	6375	St. Philip's Marsh
6308	Banbury	6376	Banbury
6309	Taunton	6377	Tyseley
6310	Neyland	6378	Swindon Works
6311	Stafford Road	6379	Gloucester
6312	Old Oak Common	6380	Old Oak Common
6313	Banbury	6381	Ebbw Junction
6314	Weston-Super-Mare	6382	Westbury
6315	Neyland	6383	Landore
6316	Banbury	6384	Westbury
6317	Ebbw Junction	6385	Reading
6318	Reading	6386	Pontypool Road
6319	Worcester	6387	Pontypool Road
6320	Shrewsbury	6388	Oxford
6321	Chester	6389	Neyland
6322	Ebbw Junction	6390	St. Philip's Marsh
6323	Banbury	6391	Old Oak Common
6324	Cheltenham High Street	6392	Old Oak Common
6325	Hereford	6393	Cardiff Canton
6326	Swindon Works	6394	Chester
6327	Banbury	6395	St. Philip's Marsh
6328	Carmarthen	6396	Tyseley
6329	Chester	6397	Weymouth
6330	Andover Junction	6398	Carmarthen
6331	Old Oak Common	6399	Shrewsbury
6332	Old Oak Common	7300	Swindon
6333	St. Philip's Marsh	7301	Tyseley
6334	Birkenhead	7302	Westbury
6335	Landore	7303	Gloucester
6336	Neyland	7304	Severn Tunnel Junction
6337	Banbury	7305	Bath Road
6338	Chester	7306	St. Philip's Marsh
6339	Birkenhead	7307	Salisbury
6340	Oxford	7308	Swindon Works
6341	Westbury	7309	Weymouth
6342	Shrewsbury	7310	Ebbw Junction
6343	Bath Road	7311	Chester
6344	Weymouth	7312	Old Oak Common
6345	Neyland	7313	Oxley
6346	Oxley	7314	Bath Road
6347	Swindon	7315	Stafford Road
6348	Chester	7316	Carmarthen
6349	Severn Tunnel Junction	7317	Shrewsbury
6350	Chester	7318	Reading
6351	Goodwick	7319	Goodwick
6352	Banbury	7320	Tyseley
6353	Worcester	7321	Oxley
6354	Swindon Stock Shed	8300	Tyseley
6355	Bath Road	8301	Swindon
6356	Cardiff Canton	8302	Oxley
6357	Reading	8304	Newton Abbot
6358	Worcester	8305	Newton Abbot
6359	Banbury	8307	Stafford Road
6360	Andover Junction	8308	Exeter
6361	Swindon F. Pool	8309	Newton Abbot
6362	Oxley	8313	Truro
6363	Swindon	8314	Bath Road
6364	Banbury	8315	Oxley

8318	Newton Abbot	8372	Truro
8320	Weymouth	8373	Old Oak Common
8322	Cardiff Canton	8374	Exeter
8325	Swindon Works	8376	Laira
8326	Severn Tunnel Junction	8378	Penzance
8327	Cardiff Canton	8379	Cardiff Canton
8328	Chester	8381	Truro
8329	Salisbury	8382	Cardiff Canton
8331	Oxley	8383	Exeter
8332	Oxley	8384	Newton Abbot
8333	Swindon Stock Shed	8386	Gloucester
8334	Birkenhead	8387	Oxley
8335	Newton Abbot	8388	Penzance
8337	Laira	8389	Ebbw Junction
8338	Newton Abbot	8390	Oxley
8340	Exeter	8391	Weymouth
8341	Oxley	8393	Stafford Road Factory
8342	Newton Abbot	9300	Reading
8343	Cardiff Canton	9301	Swindon F. Pool
8344	Oxley	9302	Reading
8350	St. Philip's Marsh	9303	Old Oak Common
8351	St. Philip's Marsh	9304	Didcot
8352	Laira	9305	Reading
8353	Laira	9306	Old Oak Common
8354	Swindon	9307	Old Oak Common
8357	Swindon	9308	Old Oak Common
8358	St. Philip's Marsh	9309	Old Oak Common
8359	Oxley	9310	Old Oak Common
8360	Ebbw Junction	9311	Old Oak Common
8361	Newton Abbot	9312	Old Oak Common
8362	Truro	9313	Old Oak Common
8363	Stafford Road	9314	Old Oak Common
8364	Swindon Works	9315	Old Oak Common
8365	Newton Abbot	9316	Southall
8366	Landore	9317	Reading
8368	Exeter	9318	Oxford
8369	Oxley	9319	Reading

2—6—4T '4400' CLASS

4400	Penzance	4406	St. Ives
4401	Laira	4407	Penzance
4402	Princetown	4408	Tondu
4403	Tondu	4409	Moorswater
4404	Penzance	4410	Newton Abbot Factory
4405	Laira		

2—6—2T '4500' CLASS

4500	Truro	4520	Ebbw Junction
4501	Tyseley	4521	St. Blazey
4502	Truro	4522	Bridgend
4503	Truro	4523	Launceston
4504	Pontypool Road	4524	Ebbw Junction
4505	Whitland	4525	Truro
4506	Whitland	4526	Swindon Works
4507	Bath Road	4527	Stourbridge
4508	St. Blazey	4528	Swindon Works
4509	Truro	4529	Aberbeeg
4510	Swindon Works	4530	Newton Abbot Factory
4511	Stourbridge	4531	Taunton
4512	Penzance	4532	Exeter
4513	Swindon Works	4533	Pontypool Road
4514	Whitland	4534	Andover Junction
4515	Whitland	4535	Moretonhampstead
4516	St. Blazey	4536	Frome
4517	St. Blazey	4537	Taunton
4518	Ebbw Junction	4538	Kingsbridge
4519	Pembroke Dock	4539	Ludlow

Small Prairie Tank No. 4562 at Gloucester shed in September 1935.
L. E. Copeland

4540	Swindon Works	4583	Newton Abbot
4541	Aberbeeg	4584	St. Blazey
4542	Kingsbridge	4585	Bath Road
4543	Newton Abbot	4586	Kidderminster
4544	Exeter	4587	Ebbw Junction
4545	Laira	4588	Bath Road
4546	Cheltenham Malv'n Rd	4589	Southall
4547	Truro	4590	Bath Road
4548	St. Blazey	4591	Laira
4549	Exeter	4592	Swindon
4550	Swindon Works	4593	Ebbw Junction
4551	Bath Road	4594	Worcester
4552	Bodmin	4595	Bath Road
4553	Landore	4596	Stafford Road Factory
4554	Exeter	4597	Pontypool Road
4555	Cheltenham Malv'n Rd	4598	Moorswater
4556	Laira	4599	Caerphilly Works
4557	Aberbeeg	5500	Southall
4558	Worcester	5501	Newton Abbot
4559	Swindon F. Pool	5502	Swindon Works
4560	Hereford	5503	Taunton
4561	Laira	5504	Newton Abbot
4562	Cheltenham Malv'n Rd	5505	Stafford Road Factory
4563	Swindon	5506	Bath Road
4564	Gloucester	5507	Swindon Works
4565	Swindon Works	5508	Cheltenham Malv'n Rd
4566	Frome	5509	Bath Road
4567	Gloucester	5510	Swindon Works
4568	Bath Road	5511	Westbury
4569	Taunton	5512	Bath Road
4570	Evesham	5513	Landore
4571	Taunton	5514	Frome
4572	Bath Road	5515	Gloucester
4573	Bath Road	5516	St. Blazey
4574	Newton Abbot	5517	Pontypool Road
4575	Aberdare	5518	Caerphilly Works
4576	Pembroke Dock	5519	Tyseley
4577	Andover Junction	5520	Aberdare
4578	Cheltenham Malv'n Rd	5521	Taunton
4579	Tyseley	5522	Swindon Works
4580	Tyseley	5523	Bath Road
4581	Taunton	5524	Kidderminster
4582	Newton Abbot	5525	Bodmin

5526	Laira	5551	Minehead
5527	Worcester	5552	Bath Road
5528	Swindon Works	5553	Bath Road
5529	Yatton	5554	Yeovil
5530	Bodmin	5555	Bath Road
5531	Cheltenham Malv'n Rd	5556	Westbury
5532	Stourbridge	5557	Newton Abbot
5533	Bridgend	5558	Bath Road
5534	Bath Road	5559	Bath
5535	Weston-Super-Mare	5560	Bath Road
5536	Bath Road	5561	Bath Road
5537	Taunton	5562	Bath Road
5538	Cheltenham Malv'n Rd	5563	Frome
5539	Whitland	5564	Wells
5540	Bath Road	5565	Bath Road
5541	Bath Road	5566	Bath Road
5542	Taunton	5567	Swindon
5543	Taunton	5568	Whitland
5544	Kidderminster	5569	Truro
5545	Aberbeeg	5570	Westbury
5546	Westbury	5571	Taunton
5547	Swindon Works	5572	Kidderminster
5548	Yeovil	5573	St. Blazey
5549	Bath Road	5574	Kidderminster
5550	Ebbw Junction		

2—8—0 '4700' CLASS

4700	Tyseley	4705	Old Oak Common
4701	Tyseley	4706	Exeter
4702	Exeter	4707	Old Oak Common
4703	Old Oak Common	4708	Old Oak Common
4704	Laira		

0—4—2T '4800' CLASS

4800	Gloucester	4808	Tiverton Junction
4801	Gloucester	4809	Exeter
4802	Lydney	4810	Croes Newydd
4803	Chalford	4811	Birkenhead
4804	Worcester	4812	Machynlleth
4805	Exeter	4813	Gloucester
4806	Exeter	4814	Alcester
4807	Exeter	4815	Oswestry

Collett 0—4—2 tank No. 4821 at Ebbw Junction shed in September 1936. No. 4821 was allocated to Pontypool Road at the start of 1934.

W. Potter

4816	Kidderminster		4823	Pontypool Road
4817	Cheltenham Malvern Rd		4824	Goodwick
4818	Worcester		4825	Staines
4819	Exeter		4826	Southall
4820	Pontrilas		4827	Reading
4821	Pontypool Road		4828	Croes Newydd
4822	Pontypool Road		4829	Westbury

0—4—2T '5800' CLASS

5800	Yatton		5810	Wellington
5801	Swindon		5811	Much Wenlock
5802	Swindon		5812	Tiverton Junction
5803	Swindon Stock Shed		5813	Ludlow
5804	Malmesbury		5814	Kington
5805	Swindon		5815	Leominster
5806	Swindon		5816	Llanfyllin
5807	Kington		5817	Worcester
5808	Worcester		5818	Ebbw Junction
5809	Croes Newydd		5819	Llandovery

4—6—0 '4900' HALL CLASS

4900	Oxford		4918	Oxley
4901	Laira		4919	Swindon Works
4902	Oxford		4920	Oxford
4903	Oxford		4921	Oxford
4904	Oxley		4922	Oxford
4905	Old Oak Common		4923	Weymouth
4906	Swindon		4924	Stafford Road
4907	Penzance		4925	Oxford
4908	Didcot		4926	Penzance
4909	Chester		4927	Cardiff Canton
4910	Penzance		4928	Swindon Stock Shed
4911	Penzance		4929	Weymouth
4912	Old Oak Common		4930	Swindon F. Pool
4913	Oxford		4931	Banbury
4914	Reading		4932	Westbury
4915	Chester		4933	Penzance
4916	Swindon Works		4934	Llanelly
4917	Stafford Road		4935	Chester

4936	Oxford		4976	Laira
4937	Swindon Works		4977	Old Oak Common
4938	Reading		4978	Banbury
4939	Carmarthen		4979	Laira
4940	Penzance		4980	Laira
4941	St. Philip's Marsh		4981	Laira
4942	Llanelly		4982	Westbury
4943	Tyseley		4983	Laira
4944	Oxford		4984	Old Oak Common
4945	St. Philip's Marsh		4985	Penzance
4946	St. Philip's Marsh		4986	Swindon Works
4947	Weymouth		4987	Old Oak Common
4948	Cardiff Canton		4988	Old Oak Common
4949	Old Oak Common		4989	Gloucester
4950	Cardiff Canton		4990	Truro
4951	Penzance		4991	Chester
4952	Tyseley		4992	Weymouth
4953	Bath Road		4993	Penzance
4954	Oxley		4994	Swindon Works
4955	Oxford		4995	Old Oak Common
4956	Bath Road		4996	Worcester
4957	Oxford		4997	Hereford
4958	Swindon Works		4998	Old Oak Common
4959	Truro		4999	Oxford
4960	Oxford		5900	Carmarthen
4961	Newton Abbot		5901	Old Oak Common
4962	Bath Road		5902	Swindon Stock Shed
4963	Reading		5903	Oxley
4964	Westbury		5904	Banbury
4965	Cardiff Canton		5905	Goodwick
4966	Laira		5906	St. Philip's Marsh
4967	Old Oak Common		5907	Chester
4968	Old Oak Common		5908	Goodwick
4969	Old Oak Common		5909	Cardiff Canton
4970	St. Philip's Marsh		5910	Old Oak Common
4971	Oxley		5911	Swindon
4972	St. Philip's Marsh		5912	Basingstoke
4973	Swindon		5913	Gloucester
4974	Oxford		5914	Reading
4975	Swindon Works		5915	Landore

'Hall' Class 4—6—0 No. 4946 *Moseley Hall* on shed at St. Philip's Marsh, Bristol, during 1934.

L & GRP, courtesy David & Charles

5916	Leamington	5929	St. Philip's Marsh
5917	St. Philip's Marsh	5930	Oxley
5918	St. Philip's Marsh	5931	Old Oak Common
5919	Weymouth	5932	Bath Road
5920	Chester	5933	Bath Road
5921	Reading	5934	Stafford Road
5922	Old Oak Common	5935	Stafford Road
5923	Old Oak Common	5936	Old Oak Common
5924	Reading	5937	Penzance
5925	Old Oak Common	5938	Stafford Road
5926	Goodwick	5939	Laira
5927	Old Oak Common	5940	Stafford Road
5928	Goodwick		

2—6—2T '5100' (ex-'3100') CLASS

5100	Tyseley	5126	Swindon Works
5111	Chester	5127	Taunton
5112	Stourbridge	5128	Stourbridge
5113	Stourbridge	5129	Wellington
5114	Banbury	5130	Stafford Road
5115	Leamington	5131	Stourbridge
5116	Stourbridge	5132	Swindon Stock Shed
5117	Tyseley	5133	Caerphilly Works
5118	St. Philip's Marsh	5134	Stratford
5119	Stafford Road Factory	5135	Stourbridge
5120	Stourbridge	5136	Chester
5121	Leamington	5137	Stourbridge
5122	Stourbridge	5138	Tyseley
5123	St. Philip's Marsh	5139	Stratford
5124	Worcester	5140	Stourbridge
5125	Stourbridge	5141	Tyseley

5142	Stourbridge	5146	Birkenhead
5143	Tyseley	5147	Birkenhead
5144	Caerphilly Works	5148	Stafford Road
5145	Stourbridge	5149	Stafford Road Factory

2—6—2T '5101' CLASS

5101	Caerphilly Works	5165	Tyseley
5102	Stourbridge	5166	Chester
5103	Tyseley	5167	Leamington
5104	Tyseley	5168	Chester
5105	Stourbridge	5169	St. Philip's Marsh
5106	Tyseley	5170	Tyseley
5107	Bath Road	5171	Leamington
5108	Stratford	5172	Taunton
5109	Caerphilly Works	5173	Stafford Road Factory
5110	St. Philip's Marsh	5174	Stafford Road
5150	Stafford Road Factory	5175	Tyseley
5151	Tyseley	5176	Birkenhead
5152	Stourbridge	5177	Stafford Road Factory
5153	Stafford Road	5178	Swindon Works
5154	Stratford	5179	Chester
5155	Leamington	5180	Tyseley
5156	Stourbridge	5181	Tyseley
5157	Tyseley	5182	Stourbridge
5158	Bath Road	5183	Stourbridge
5159	Birkenhead	5184	Chester
5160	Leamington	5185	Chester
5161	Chester	5186	Tyseley
5162	Tyseley	5187	Swindon Works
5163	Tyseley	5188	Stourbridge
5164	Stafford Road	5189	Caerphilly Works

0—6—0T '5400' CLASS

5400	Southall	5410	Southall
5401	Southall	5411	Cathays
5402	Frome	5412	Southall
5403	Frome	5413	Southall
5404	Stafford Road	5414	Swindon Works
5405	Banbury	5415	Southall
5406	Swindon Works	5416	Southall
5407	Banbury	5417	Southall
5408	Southall	5418	Southall
5409	Southall	5419	Westbury

5658	Cathays	5699	Barry
5659	Treherbert	6600	St. Philip's Marsh
5660	Rhymney	6601	Duffryn Yard
5661	Merthyr	6602	Shrewsbury
5662	Caerphilly*	6603	Duffryn Yard
5663	Swindon Stock Shed*	6604	Duffryn Yard
5664	Barry	6605	Caerphilly Works
5665	Treherbert	6606	Cathays
5666	Barry	6607	Radyr Junction
5667	Ferndale	6608	Radyr Junction
5668	Cae Harris	6609	Radyr Junction

Locomotive No. 6600 stands at the front of St. Philip's Marsh shed, Bristol, its home shed, during 1934.

L & GRP, courtesy David & Charles

0—6—2T '5600' CLASS

5600	Barry	5629	Ferndale
5601	Treherbert	5630	Barry Factory
5602	Barry	5631	Swindon Stock Shed*
5603	Barry Factory	5632	Swindon Stock Shed*
5604	Swindon Stock Shed*	5633	Swindon Stock Shed*
5605	Barry	5634	Swindon Stock Shed*
5606	Ferndale	5635	Coke Ovens
5607	Cathays	5636	Treherbert
5608	Treherbert	5637	Abercynon
5609	Landore	5638	Swindon Stock Shed*
5610	Barry	5639	Treherbert
5611	Treherbert	5640	Treherbert
5612	Swindon Stock Shed*	5641	Caerphilly Works
5613	Swindon Stock Shed*	5642	Coke Ovens
5614	Duffryn Yard	5643	Coke Ovens
5615	Treherbert	5644	Caerphilly Works
5616	Ferndale	5645	Swindon Stock Shed*
5617	Ferndale	5646	Treherbert
5618	Abercynon	5647	Cae Harris
5619	Abercynon	5648	Ferndale
5620	Ferndale	5649	Swindon Stock Shed*
5621	Barry	5650	Landore
5622	Barry	5651	Cathays
5623	Ferndale	5652	Cae Harris
5624	Barry	5653	Cae Harris
5625	Severn Tunnel Junct.	5654	Cae Harris
5626	Severn Tunnel Junct.	5655	Rhymney
5627	Treherbert	5656	Swindon Stock Shed*
5628	Swindon Stock Shed*	5657	Swindon Stock Shed*

5669	Coke Ovens	6610	Radyr Junction
5670	Cardiff Canton	6611	Barry
5671	Merthyr	6612	Barry
5672	Merthyr	6613	Cathays
5673	Swindon Works	6614	Barry
5674	Coke Ovens	6615	Cathays
5675	Swindon Stock Shed*	6616	Cathays
5676	Treherbert	6617	Cathays
5677	Merthyr	6618	Cathays
5678	Merthyr	6619	Barry
5679	Cardiff Canton	6620	Barry
5680	Treherbert	6621	Ebbw Junction
5681	Cathays	6622	Caerphilly Works
5682	Coke Ovens	6623	Reading
5683	Rhymney	6624	Chester
5684	Abercynon	6625	Shrewsbury
5685	Aberbeeg	6626	Cathays
5686	Abercynon	6627	Cathays
5687	Treherbert	6628	Cathays
5688	Swansea East Dock	6629	Cathays
5689	Westbury	6630	Croes Newydd
5690	Rhymney	6631	Oxford
5691	Treherbert	6632	Banbury
5692	Rhymney	6633	Duffryn Yard
5693	Barry	6634	Swindon Works
5694	Cae Harris	6635	Cathays
5695	Treherbert	6636	Pontypool Road
5696	Rhymney	6637	Radyr Junction
5697	Landore	6638	Landore
5698	Treherbert	6639	Severn Tunnel Junction

* Stored

6640 Cathays	6670 Barry	5772 Old Oak Common	6740 Swindon
6641 Barry	6671 Barry	5773 Old Oak Common	6741 Swindon
6642 Cardiff Canton	6672 Ebbw Junction	5774 St. Philip's Marsh	6742 Branches Fork
6643 Barry	6673 St. Philip's Marsh	5775 Neath	6743 Ebbw Junction
6644 Barry	6674 Swindon Stock Shed*	5776 Tondu	6744 Stafford Road
6645 Cathays	6675 Cardiff Canton	5777 Llantrisant	6745 Tyseley
6646 Barry	6676 Swindon Stock Shed	5778 Neath	6746 Tyseley
6647 Barry	6677 Swansea East Dock	5779 Old Oak Common	6747 Tyseley
6648 Croes Newydd	6678 Caerphilly Works	5780 Oxley	6748 Stourbridge
6649 Caerphilly Works	6679 Duffryn Yard	5781 St. Philip's Marsh	6749 Oxley
6650 Cardiff Canton	6680 Neath	5782 Llanelly	7700 Swindon F. Pool
6651 Cardiff Canton	6681 Landore	5783 Ebbw Junction	7701 Neath
6652 Aberdare	6682 Llanelly	5784 St. Philip's Marsh	7702 Llanelly
6653 Cathays	6683 Landore	5785 St. Philip's Marsh	7703 Banbury
6654 Aberbeeg	6684 Swansea East Dock	5786 Aberdare	7704 Duffryn Yard
6655 Cathays	6685 Ebbw Junction	5787 Severn Tunnel Junction	7705 Stafford Road
6656 Pontypool Road	6686 Duffryn Yard	5788 Aberbeeg	7706 Stafford Road Factory
6657 Radyr Junction	6687 Pontypool Road	5789 Ebbw Junction	7707 Hereford
6658 Cathays	6688 Duffryn Yard	5790 Stourbridge	7708 Reading
6659 Cathays	6689 Ebbw Junction	5791 Stourbridge	7709 Old Oak Common
6660 Cathays	6690 Westbury	5792 Tondu	7710 Oxford
6661 Cathays	6691 Severn Tunnel Junct.	5793 Gloucester	7711 Westbury
6662 Cathays	6692 Cardiff Canton	5794 Stourbridge	7712 Tondu
6663 Merthyr	6693 Ebbw Junction	5795 Stourbridge	7713 Old Oak Common
6664 Cathays	6694 Croes Newydd	5796 Llantrisant	7714 Tyseley
6665 Chester	6695 Leamington	5797 Tondu	7715 St. Blazey
6666 Cardiff Canton	6696 Leamington	5798 Old Oak Common	7716 St. Blazey
6667 Barry	6697 Leamington	5799 Old Oak Common	7717 Merthyr
6668 Barry	6698 Croes Newydd	6700 Cardiff East Dock	7718 St. Philip's Marsh
6669 Barry	6699 Banbury	6701 Cardiff East Dock	7719 St. Philip's Marsh

0–6–0T '5700' CLASS

5700 Banbury	5736 Banbury	6702 Cardiff East Dock	7720 Tondu
5701 Oxley	5737 Old Oak Common	6703 Cardiff East Dock	7721 Tondu
5702 Neath & Brecon	5738 Tyseley	6704 Cardiff East Dock	7722 Aberbeeg
5703 Glyn Neath	5739 Oxley	6705 Cardiff East Dock	7723 Gloucester
5704 Swansea East Dock	5740 Llantrisant	6706 Cardiff East Dock	7724 Gloucester
5705 Swansea East Dock	5741 Aberbeeg	6707 Cardiff East Dock	7725 Tondu
5706 Llantrisant	5742 Tyseley	6708 Cardiff East Dock	7726 Westbury
5707 Tondu	5743 Swansea East Dock	6709 Cardiff East Dock	7727 Westbury
5708 Tondu	5744 Southall	6710 St. Philip's Marsh	7728 Swindon
5709 Tondu	5745 Old Oak Common	6711 Swindon	7729 St. Philip's Marsh
5710 Cardiff Canton	5746 Glyn Neath	6712 Westbury	7730 Westbury
5711 Merthyr	5747 Aberdare	6713 Swansea East Dock	7731 Slough
5712 Oxley	5748 Pontypool Road	6714 Swansea East Dock	7732 Old Oak Common
5713 Ebbw Junction	5749 Ebbw Junction	6715 Swansea East Dock	7733 Duffryn
5714 Aberdare	5750 Old Oak Common	6716 St. Philip's Marsh	7734 Old Oak Common
5715 Old Oak Common	5751 Old Oak Common	6717 Duffryn Yard	7735 St. Philip's Marsh
5716 St. Philip's Marsh	5752 Old Oak Common	6718 Duffryn Yard	7736 Tondu
5717 Old Oak Common	5753 Old Oak Common	6719 Duffryn Yard	7737 Neath
5718 Westbury	5754 Old Oak Common	6720 Duffryn Yard	7738 Landore
5719 Oxley	5755 Cardiff East Dock	6721 Stourbridge	7739 Neath & Brecon
5720 Neath & Brecon	5756 Cardiff Canton	6722 Chester	7740 Duffryn Yard
5721 Merthyr	5757 Old Oak Common	6723 Chester	7741 Gloucester
5722 Llanelly & Mynydd Mawr	5758 Old Oak Common	6724 Swindon	7742 Neath
5723 Banbury	5759 Old Oak Common	6725 Ebbw Junction Shops	7743 Neath
5724 Tyseley	5760 Swindon Works	6726 Pill	7744 Duffryn Yard
5725 Tyseley	5761 Old Oak Common	6727 Pill	7745 Llanelly
5726 Tyseley	5762 Old Oak Common	6728 Pill	7746 Caerphilly Works
5727 Old Oak Common	5763 Old Oak Common	6729 Pill	7747 Aberdare
5728 Pontypool Road	5764 Old Oak Common	6730 Pill	7748 Tondu
5729 Aberdare	5765 Old Oak Common	6731 Pill	7749 Westbury
5730 Caerphilly Works	5766 Old Oak Common	6732 Pill	7750 Old Oak Common
5731 Llanelly	5767 Old Oak Common	6733 Swindon	7751 Pontypool Road
5732 Barry Factory	5768 Aberdare	6734 Swindon	7752 Aberdare
5733 Ebbw Junction	5769 Merthyr	6735 Swindon	7753 Duffryn Yard
5734 Neath & Brecon	5770 St. Philip's Marsh	6736 Swindon	7754 Henley
5735 Reading	5771 St. Philip's Marsh	6737 Swindon	7755 Swansea East Dock
		6738 Swindon	7756 Duffryn Yard
		6739 Swindon	7757 Neath & Brecon

*Stored

Various tank engines and a Churchward mogul can be seen outside the repair shops at Ebbw Junction shed in September 1936. Locomotives which can be identified are 0—6—0 pannier tanks Nos. 7752 and 1759, which were allocated to Aberdare and Ebbw Junction respectively at the start of 1934.   *W. Potter*

'King' Class 4—6—0 No. 6015 *King Richard III* stands in front of the coaling stage at Old Oak Common during 1934.   *Photomatic*

7758	Tyseley	8719	Newton Abbot
7759	Oxley	8720	Danygraig
7760	Laira	8721	Llantrisant
7761	Exeter	8722	Westbury
7762	St. Philip's Marsh	8723	Aberbeeg
7763	Oxley	8724	Pontypool Road
7764	Cardiff Canton	8725	Stourbridge
7765	Oswestry	8726	Tyseley
7766	Merthyr	8727	Swindon Works
7767	Neath	8728	Aberbeeg
7768	Pontypool Road	8729	Swindon F. Pool
7769	Caerphilly Works	8730	St. Philip's Marsh
7770	Gloucester	8731	Kidderminster
7771	Ebbw Junction	8732	Danygraig
7772	Merthyr	8733	St. Philip's Marsh
7773	Aberdare	8734	Chester
7774	Aberbeeg	8735	Ebbw Junction
7775	Barry Factory	8736	Merthyr
7776	Ebbw Junction	8737	Brecon
7777	Ebbw Junction	8738	Cardiff Canton
7778	Swindon Works	8739	Ebbw Junction
7779	Swindon Works	8740	Reading
7780	Landore	8741	Swindon
7781	Ebbw Junction	8742	Reading
7782	St. Philip's Marsh	8743	Swindon Works
7783	St. Philip's Marsh	8744	Westbury
7784	St. Philip's Marsh	8745	Frome
7785	Swansea East Dock	8746	St. Philip's Marsh
7786	Neath	8747	St. Philip's Marsh
7787	Duffryn Yard	8748	Ebbw Junction
7788	Reading	8749	Landore
7789	Swindon Works	8750	Old Oak Common
7790	St. Philip's Marsh	8751	Old Oak Common
7791	Swindon Works	8752	Old Oak Common
7792	St. Philip's Marsh	8753	Old Oak Common
7793	Bath	8754	Old Oak Common
7794	St. Philip's Marsh	8755	Old Oak Common
7795	St. Philip's Marsh	8756	Old Oak Common
7796	Shrewsbury	8757	Southall
7797	Tyseley	8758	Southall
7798	Swindon Stock Shed	8759	Old Oak Common
7799	Swindon Works	8760	Old Oak Common
8700	Swindon Works	8761	Old Oak Common
8701	Kidderminster	8762	Old Oak Common
8702	Swindon	8763	Old Oak Common
8703	St. Philip's Marsh	8764	Old Oak Common
8704	Chester	8765	Swindon Stock Shed
8705	Chester	8766	Reading
8706	Llanelly	8767	Old Oak Common
8707	Pantyffynnon	8768	Didcot
8708	Llanelly	8769	Old Oak Common
8709	Exeter	9701	Old Oak Common
8710	Severn Tunnel Junction	9702	Old Oak Common
8711	Swindon Works	9703	Old Oak Common
8712	Pontypool Road	9704	Old Oak Common
8713	St. Philip's Marsh	9705	Old Oak Common
8714	St. Philip's Marsh	9706	Old Oak Common
8715	Llanelly	9707	Old Oak Common
8716	Severn Tunnel Junction	9708	Old Oak Common
8717	Worcester	9709	Old Oak Common
8718	Gloucester	9710	Old Oak Common

4—6—0 '6000' KING CLASS

6000	Old Oak Common	6005	Stafford Road
6001	Old Oak Common	6006	Stafford Road
6002	Laira	6007	Old Oak Common
6003	Old Oak Common	6008	Stafford Road
6004	Laira	6009	Old Oak Common

6010	Laira	6020	Laira
6011	Swindon Works	6021	Old Oak Common
6012	Laira	6022	Laira
6013	Old Oak Common	6023	Newton Abbot
6014	Stafford Road	6024	Laira
6015	Old Oak Common	6025	Old Oak Common
6016	Laira	6026	Swindon Works
6017	Swindon Stock Shed	6027	Old Oak Common
6018	Swindon Works	6028	Old Oak Common
6019	Stafford Road	6029	Old Oak Common

2—6—2T '6100' CLASS

6100	Slough	6130	Slough
6101	Swindon Works	6131	Reading
6102	Old Oak Common	6132	Reading
6103	Old Oak Common	6133	Southall
6104	Slough	6134	Aylesbury
6105	Swindon Stock Shed	6135	Aylesbury
6106	Old Oak Common	6136	Slough
6107	Southall	6137	Old Oak Common
6108	Old Oak Common	6138	Reading
6109	Reading	6139	Southall
6110	Reading	6140	Reading
6111	Swindon Works	6141	Old Oak Common
6112	Southall	6142	Slough
6113	Slough	6143	Old Oak Common
6114	Slough	6144	Old Oak Common
6115	Swindon Works	6145	Slough
6116	Slough	6146	Slough
6117	Basingstoke	6147	Southall
6118	Slough	6148	Southall
6119	Slough	6149	Slough
6120	Slough	6150	Slough
6121	Slough	6151	Old Oak Common
6122	Old Oak Common	6152	Slough
6123	Slough	6153	Southall
6124	Slough	6154	Reading
6125	Old Oak Common	6155	Slough
6126	Old Oak Common	6156	Southall
6127	Aylesbury	6157	Slough
6128	Southall	6158	Slough
6129	Slough	6159	Southall

0—6—0T '6400' CLASS

6400	Aberdare	6405	Stourbridge
6401	Merthyr	6406	Swindon Works
6402	Cardiff Canton	6407	Plymouth
6403	Stafford Road	6408	Laira
6404	Stourbridge	6409	Laira

DIESEL RAILCAR

1	Southall

STEAM RAILMOTORS

30	Southall	78	Croes Newydd
37	Reading	79	Swindon Stock Shed
55	Swindon F. Pool	80	Exeter
64	Stourbridge	81	St. Philip's Marsh
65	Swindon F. Pool	88	Swindon F. Pool
66	Stourbridge	91	Southall
70	Neath	92	Southall
71	Swindon Works	93	Stourbridge
72	Swindon Stock Shed	96	Exeter
75	Swindon Stock Shed	97	Swindon F. Pool
76	St. Philip's Marsh	98	Swindon Stock Shed
77	St. Philip's Marsh		

The new GWR shed at Abercynon (formerly Taff Vale Railway) on 21st July 1935. On shed on this occasion were 5618, 5635, 5686, 5642, 5669, 5682, 5630, 5637, 414, 401, 352, 398, 337, 380, 3595, 1234, 351, 356, 402, 58, 57, 288, 289, 268, and 397.

W. A. Camwell

SHED ALLOCATIONS

ABERAYRON

205   548

ABERBEEG

1505 1580 1615 1801 1884 2736 2769 4233 4243 4290 4529 4541 4557 5545 5685 5741 5788 6654 7722 7774 8723 8728

ABERCYNON

238   267   268   278   287   288   289   299   337   5618 5619 5637 5684 5686

ABERDARE

282   294   296   302   311   362   374   1272 1420 1454 1530 1535 1718 1737 1769 1839 2454 2484 2667 2739 2742 2793 2804 2808 2809 2810 2813 2821 2832 2849 2857 2862 2866 2869 2880 3036 4228 4261 4285 4294 4297 4300 4575 5204 5233 5255 5271 5520 5714 5729 5747 5768 5786 6400 6652 7747 7752 7773

ABERYSTWYTH

875   1954 2012 2321 2421 2424 2438 2445 2466 3255 3262 3264 3271 3272 3275 3288

ABERYSTWYTH (Narrow Gauge)

7   8   1213

ABINGDON

1427

ALCESTER

4814

ANDOVER JUNCTION

3278 3289 4534 4577 6330 6360

ASHBURTON

1443

AYLESBURY

1438 6127 6134 6135

BALA

759   1136 1410 1776

BANBURY

216   1237 2368 2385 2531 2539 2606 2607 2610 2673 2713 2817 2872 3150 3370 3387 3395 3399 3445 4324 4361 4931 4978 5114 5311 5324 5405 5407 5700 5723 5736 5904 6308 6313 6316 6323 6327 6337 6352 6359 6364 6369 6376 6632 6699 7703

Bala shed on 4th September 1938 with 5810 and 1524 outside and 2419 and 7403 inside.

W. A. Camwell

Dowlais (Cae Harris) on
21st July 1935.
W. A. Camwell

BARNSTAPLE
3416 3444 4391

BARRY

52	55	58	59	66	154	210	212	224	229
231	234	235	242	243	244	248	252	253	254
256	257	258	259	260	261	262	263	264	265
266	269	270	271	272	273	274	275	276	277
345	361	377	379	384	386	387	388	389	394
404	439	440	441	782	783	784	4231	4240	4251
5201	5203	5207	5208	5224	5225	5244	5251	5600	5602
5605	5610	5621	5622	5624	5664	5666	5693	5699	6611
6612	6614	6619	6620	6641	6643	6644	6646	6647	6667
6668	6669	6670	6671						

BARRY WORKS
247   372   1278   1890   2123   2738   5603   5630   5732   7775

BASINGSTOKE
4320 5912 6117

BATH
5559 7793

BATH ROAD, BRISTOL

1938	2013	2381	2441	2526	2908	2923	2940	2949	2971
3300	3305	3367	3376	3378	3379	3396	3430	3433	3446
3452	4010	4012	4016	4023	4028	4035	4039	4043	4053
4061	4076	4369	4507	4551	4568	4572	4573	4585	4588
4590	4595	4953	4956	4962	5107	5158	5506	5509	5512
5523	5534	5536	5540	5541	5549	5552	5553	5555	5558
5560	5561	5562	5565	5566	5932	5933	6303	6305	6343
6355	7305	7314	8314						

BATH ROAD WORKS
2543

BIRKENHEAD
646 1532 1545 1712 1808 1810 1904 1917 1943 1959
2005 2055 2065 2067 2071 2090 2095 2120 2702 3575
3577 3578 3579 3580 3627 4317 4351 4811 5146 5147
5159 5176 5346 6300 6334 6339 8334

BODMIN
4552 5525 5530

BRANCHES FORK
1888 6742

BRECON
1531 2327 2336 2342 2412 2459 2516 2559 2715 8737

BRIDGEND
949 1645 4522 5533

BRIDGWATER
870

BRIDPORT
1239 1289

BRIMSCOMBE
3171

BUILTH WELLS
2405

BURRY PORT
1907 1929 1936 1937 1978 1979 2002 2163 2165 2167
2168 2193 2198

CAE HARRIS
138   139 5647 5652 5653 5654 5668 5694

CAERPHILLY WORKS

293	357	370	382	577	1889	1971	3573	4208	4249
4280	4599	5101	5109	5133	5144	5189	5211	5256	5270
5273	5518	5641	5644	5730	6605	6622	6649	6678	7746
7769									

CARDIFF CANTON

236	280	283	284	286	300	310	313	314	317
318	349	381	410	411	420	487	584	1285	1585
1685	1775	1791	1868	1931	1966	1990	1998	2035	2048
2049	2058	2113	2124	2136	2141	2143	2150	2433	2470
2478	2524	2548	2612	2635	2646	2653	2654	2671	2672
2726	2762	2767	2917	2922	2972	2975	2983	2988	2990
3002	3041	3156	3168	3185	3386	3392	3407	3411	3419
3422	3594	4009	4081	4084	4093	4099	4239	4241	4242
4258	4278	4319	4344	4360	4367	4378	4927	4948	4950
4965	5004	5012	5205	5257	5670	5679	5710	5756	5909
6356	6393	6402	6642	6650	6651	6666	6675	6692	7764
8322	8327	8343	8379	8382	8738				

CARDIFF, EAST DOCK

31	37	53	54	56	57	67	72	155	295
297	319	604	605	606	608	609	610	611	681
682	683	684	717	718	721	780	1928	1970	2000
2022	2086	5755	6700	6701	6702	6703	6704	6705	6706
6707	6708	6709							

CARDIGAN

1923

CARMARTHEN

559	762	845	1826	1957	1963	1982	2011	2027	2056
2085	2111	2396	2407	2418	2422	2440	2465	2474	2487
2572	2580	2640	3042	3044	3344	3390	3415	3425	3455
4037	4085	4939	5900	6328	6365	6398	7316		

CATHAYS

30	33	38	40	51	74	291	292	320	324
343	346	347	348	360	364	367	371	375	376
383	390	391	393	403	406	506	714	719	723
725	1234	2142	5411	5607	5651	5658	5681	6606	6613
6615	6616	6617	6618	6626	6627	6628	6629	6635	6640
6645	6653	6655	6658	6659	6660	6661	6662	6664	

CHALFORD

4803

CHELTENHAM (High Street)

1122 1123 1128 2619 3268 6324 6371

CHELTENHAM (Malvern Road)

4546 4555 4562 4578 4817 5508 5531 5538

CHESTER

766	767	1492	1773	1785	1802	1947	2270	2436	2464
2511	2554	2579	2623	2650	2658	2665	2674	2711	2777
2916	2936	2950	3327	3359	3442	3604	3618	4323	4330
4339	4346	4376	4909	4915	4935	4991	5111	5136	5161
5166	5168	5179	5184	5185	5345	5348	5349	5907	5920
6321	6329	6338	6348	6350	6394	6624	6665	6722	6723
7311	8328	8704	8705	8734					

CHIPPENHAM

525 528 1444 2023 2060 2064 2415

CIRENCESTER

992

CLEOBURY MORTIMER

No allocation

COKE OVENS

298	351	352	356	380	397	398	401	402	414
573	3595	3597	3599	5635	5642	5643	5669	5674	5682

CORRIS (Narrow Gauge)

3   4

CREWE

3405

CROES NEWYDD

45	96	1080	1482	1488	1511	1539	1960	2076	2129
2135	2144	2427	2555	2617	2642	2679	3211	3219	3566
4347	4810	4828	5809	6630	6648	6694	6698		

Steam Railmotor   78

DANYGRAIG

167	169	177	178	438	803	805	989	1085	1086
1101	1102	1103	1105	1106	1393	1568	1861	1883	1893
2196	2707	4207	4256	4283	5217	8720	8732		

DIDCOT

908	1159	1334	1335	1610	1848	1912	1969	2045	2190
2225	2254	2259	2395	2397	2430	2450	2463	2532	2549
3256	3267	3279	3280	3282	3290	3324	3361	3380	3385
3448	3454	4908	8768	9304					

DOWLAIS

78   82

DUFFRYN

164	171	172	173	179	184	186	187	188	733
802	806	812	813	1145	1358	1359	1704	1732	1733
1740	1754	1756	1768	1844	2630	2638	2722	2741	2746
2751	2792	4246	4274	5210	5237	5258	5274	5614	6601
6603	6604	6633	6679	6686	6688	6717	6718	6719	6720
7704	7733	7740	7744	7753	7756	7787			

EBBW JUNCTION, NEWPORT

21	332	566	753	971	975	1019	1154	1181	1256
1265	1268	1284	1292	1372	1373	1374	1375	1445	1552
1593	1647	1668	1670	1720	1723	1734	1735	1752	1759
1800	1820	1823	1846	1896	2008	2033	2053	2063	2073
2122	2154	2186	2540	2546	2571	2601	2651	2724	2734
2764	2794	2795	2811	2902	2948	2982	3161	3162	3170
4203	4205	4206	4216	4220	4224	4226	4234	4235	4247
4253	4269	4270	4271	4276	4279	4284	4286	4289	4291
4301	4318	4334	4372	4518	4520	4524	4587	4593	5200
5206	5218	5222	5234	5236	5238	5240	5241	5243	5245
5248	5249	5252	5259	5260	5261	5267	5310	5336	5398
5550	5713	5733	5749	5783	5789	5818	6317	6322	6381
6621	6672	6685	6689	6693	6743	7310	7771	7776	7777
7781	8360	8389	8735	8739	8748				

Evesham on 13th June 1937 with 2557 and 4558 outside and 4546 inside.

W. A. Camwell

Nos. 5216, 5242, 7757 (inside), 7737 and 5217 at Glyn Neath on 6th September 1936.

W. A. Camwell

EBBW JUNCTION WORKS
1862 1894 2399 3043 6725

EVESHAM
2536 4570

EXETER
1148 1300 1617 1717 1753 1897 1930 1992 2050 2103
2127 2647 2676 3031 3336 4007 4024 4026 4045 4054
4056 4532 4544 4549 4554 4702 4706 4805 4806 4807
4809 4819 7761 8308 8340 8368 8374 8383 8709
Steam railmotors   80   96

FAIRFORD
3585 3588

FERNDALE
 290   301   321   430 5606 5616 5617 5620 5623 5629
5648 5667

FROME
2705 2799 4536 4566 5402 5403 5514 5563 8745

GLOUCESTER
1003 1005 1006 1009 1010 1126 1415 1459 1538 2051
2091 2099 2100 2131 2147 2149 2153 2258 2384 2392
2398 2402 2605 2627 2670 2680 2768 2921 2944 2951
2980 3029 3048 3164 3173 3260 3261 3285 3314 3322
3420 3440 3451 3561 4306 4564 4567 4800 4801 4813
4989 5394 5515 5793 5913 6379 7303 7723 7724 7741
7770 8386 8718

GLYN NEATH
4254 5216 5254 5703 5746

GOODWICK
 215   637   639   640   848   983 1468 1597 4824 5395
5905 5908 5926 5928 6304 6351 7319

HELSTON
1496

HENLEY
7754

HEREFORD
 828 1502 1919 2020 2029 2040 2138 2479 2519 2661
2931 2978 3307 3308 3318 3328 3337 3349 3350 3355
3372 3388 3402 3409 3427 3436 4560 4997 5385 6325
7707

HONEYBOURNE
2375

KIDDERMINSTER
  28   29 1169 1254 1898 3557 4586 4816 5524 5544
5572 5574 8701 8731

KINGHAM
1004

KINGSBRIDGE
4538 4542

Llantrisant on 24th July 1938 when the following were present: (front) 4288, 5708, 4208, 8721, 3584, 3586, 5235, (at rear) 5710, 3594, 4200, 1795, 5777, 7751, 1718, 3703, 247 and 5713.

W. A. Camwell

KINGTON
533 5807 5814

LAIRA
1271 1364 1658 1755 1761 1905 1909 1922 1973 1985
1999 2148 2602 2648 2660 2812 2819 2846 2871 3049
3160 3180 3181 3342 3393 3398 3401 3424 4032 4077
4080 4094 4401 4405 4545 4556 4561 4591 4704 4901
4966 4976 4979 4980 4981 4983 5000 5006 5009 5013
5020 5021 5526 5939 6002 6004 6010 6012 6016 6020
6022 6024 6408 6409 7760 8337 8352 8353 8376

LAMBOURN
1935

LANDORE
738 1235 1719 1837 2446 2643 2842 2860 3003 3907
3916 4004 4017 4018 4019 4027 4030 4040 4042 4047
4057 4059 4070 4074 4223 4282 4322 4553 5209 5230
5246 5250 5513 5609 5650 5697 5915 6301 6302 6335
6383 6638 6681 6683 7738 7780 8366 8749

LAUNCESTON
4523

LEAMINGTON
354 1157 1260 1276 1542 2356 2918 3163 3628 5115
5121 5155 5160 5167 5171 5916 6695 6696 6697

LEDBURY
1741 1796 1864

LEOMINSTER
1706 3574 5815

LLANDOVERY
2558 5819

LLANELLY
312 339 704 752 872 997 1279 1762 1855 1858
1866 1941 1948 1975 1988 1991 2018 2042 2083 2137
2162 2176 2197 2360 2372 2382 2600 2625 2628 2631
2645 2657 2721 2800 2807 2825 2858 2877 3004 3009
3015 3028 3034 4204 4212 4213 4277 4281 4292 4296
4934 4942 5213 5263 5265 5371 5731 5782 6367 6682
7702 7745 8706 8708 8715

LLANELLY AND MYNYDD MAWR
859 1942 1974 5722

LLANFYLLIN
5816

LLANIDLOES
2417 2483 2514 2522

LLANTRISANT
617 967 1161 1408 1485 1493 1642 1649 1713 1795
2082 2759 2770 2773 3584 4257 4266 4287 4288 5706
5740 5777 5796 8721

LUDLOW
1783 4539 5813

Leominster with 5807, 5817, 2400 and 2458 on 28th June 1936.   *W. A. Camwell*

LYDNEY
2024 2025 2039 2041 2043 2070 2084 2088 2093 2118
2146 2151 2155 2156 2157 2349 2428 4802

MACHYNLLETH
884 893 894 898 1924 2313 2341 2343 2345 2352
2353 2449 2455 2490 3206 3213 3225 3257 3270 3287
4812

MALMESBURY
5804

MARLOW
1404 3583

MERTHYR
344 1247 1470 1486 1495 1707 1721 1827 1838 1873
1878 1887 2066 2732 2750 2760 2766 2781 5661 5671
5672 5677 5678 5711 5721 5769 6401 6663 7717 7766
7772 8736

MILFORD HAVEN
1641 1854

MINEHEAD
5551

MOAT LANE
819 876 ᵎ885 2068 2316 2401 2447

MOORSWATER
4409 4598

MORETONHAMPSTEAD
4535

MUCH WENLOCK

1779 5811

NEATH

558 906 1142 1637 1806 1867 2192 2390 2411 2530
2700 2763 2775 2797 2806 2882 3000 3006 3010 3901
4219 4259 4265 4366 4394 5215 5239 5268 5775 5778
6680 7701 7737 7742 7743 7767 7786
Steam Railmotor 70

NEATH AND BRECON

1608 1611 1630 1715 1727 1882 2756 2796 5702 5720
5734 7739 7757

NEWBURY

2533

NEWCASTLE EMLYN

538

NEWTON ABBOT

470 830 831 1162 1282 1362 1487 1702 1729 1876
1895 2709 2737 2864 2881 3032 3029 3151 3152 3153
3155 3166 3183 3184 3313 3357 3443 4088 4091 4543
4574 4582 4583 4961 5010 5011 5014 5016 5019 5501
5504 5557 6023 8304 8305 8309 8318 8335 8338 8342
8361 8365 8384 8719

NEWTON ABBOT WORKS

1500 1562 3587 4410 4530

NEYLAND

2618 3011 3397 3400 3435 3437 3447 4311 4331 4340
4352 4356 4382 4399 5347 6310 6315 6336 6345 6389

OLD OAK COMMON

13 111 634 642 643 1903 1946 2026 2038 2222
2226 2239 2246 2250 2303 2362 2370 2443 2611 2668
2801 2805 2816 2847 2855 2856 2865 2867 2879 3047
3567 3568 3570 3586 3591 3592 3610 4000 4003 4005
4008 4015 4020 4036 4050 4052 4071 4073 4075 4078
4082 4083 4087 4098 4341 4345 4363 4703 4705 4707
4708 4905 4912 4949 4967 4968 4969 4977 4984 4987
4988 4995 4998 5001 5003 5007 5008 5015 5017 5018
5380 5715 5717 5727 5737 5745 5750 5751 5752 5753
5754 5757 5758 5759 5761 5762 5763 5764 5765 5766
5767 5772 5773 5779 5798 5799 5901 5910 5922 5923
5925 5927 5931 5936 6000 6001 6003 6007 6009 6013
6015 6021 6025 6027 6028 6029 6102 6103 6106 6108
6122 6125 6126 6137 6141 6143 6144 6151 6312 6331
6332 6380 6391 6392 7312 7709 7713 7732 7734 7750
8373 8750 8751 8752 8753 8754 8755 8756 8759 8760
8761 8762 8763 8764 8767 8769 9303 9306 9307 9308
9309 9310 9311 9312 9313 9314 9315 9701 9702 9703
9704 9705 9706 9707 9708 9709 9710

OSWESTRY

522 523 824 837 844 849 873 878 880 882
887 895 896 900 910 1164 1196 1197 1308 1376
1478 1533 2032 2054 2075 2337 2339 2354 2457 2545
2556 2574 3253 3254 3258 3263 3265 3269 3284 4815
7765

OSWESTRY WORKS

680 2523

OXFORD

457 1134 1250 1473 1565 1574 1751 1872 1958 2332
2429 2609 2863 3325 3429 3589 4900 4902 4903 4913
4920 4921 4922 4925 4936 4944 4955 4957 4960 4974
4999 6340 6388 6631 7710 9318

OXLEY

1072 1195 1745 1747 2389 2406 2408 2451 2452 2513
2622 2633 2641 2733 2778 2818 3024 3030 3033 3040
4316 4337 4342 4353 4357 4358 4385 4389 4390 4395
4396 4904 4918 4954 4971 5370 5392 5399 5701 5712
5719 5739 5780 5903 5930 6346 6362 6366 6374 6749
7313 7321 7759 7763 8302 8315 8331 8332 8341 8344
8359 8369 8387 8390

PANTYFFYNNON

770 1287 1546 1638 1798 1814 1818 1859 2730 2782
2790 2798 2844 5212 5219 5220 5226 5228 5247 8707

PEMBROKE DOCK

4519 4576

PENMAENPOOL

1430

PENZANCE

2097 2116 2125 4400 4404 4407 4512 4907 4910 4911
4926 4933 4940 4951 4985 4993 5937 8378 8388

PILL, NEWPORT

11 190 191 192 504 666 667 671 698 850
888 1084 1113 1205 1206 1226 1726 1891 2037 2098
2728 2731 2749 2754 4201 4211 4225 4229 4236 4238
4268 4273 4275 4299 5266 6726 6727 6728 6729 6730
6731 6732

PLYMOUTH

1167 1361 1363 1365 6407

PONTRILAS

4820

PONTYPOOL ROAD

335 385 743 963 1245 1269 1534 1600 1705 1722
1730 1849 2009 2021 2034 2077 2080 2094 2117 2132
2133 2140 2159 2160 2434 2573 2608 2616 2637 2649
2656 2723 2788 2828 2829 2830 2838 2841 2850 2905
2947 3018 3023 3037 3038 3339 4260 4264 4302 4303
4325 4335 4371 4388 4397 4504 4533 4597 4821 4822
4823 5316 5517 5728 5748 6386 6387 6636 6656 6687
7751 7768 8712 8724

PORTMADOC

864 2323 2468 2520 2576 3217

PRINCETOWN

4402

PWLLHELI

2315 2553 2560

RADYR JUNCTION

32 35 36 41 43 44 47 48 49 50
198 200 206 207 213 214 226 227 230 240
246 250 1341 6607 6608 6609 6610 6637 6657

Nos. 2435, 2289, 4834 and 2378 (inside) at Penmaenpool on 16th August 1936. *W. A. Camwell*

Golden Valley branch locomotive No. 5818 outside Pontrilas shed on 20th July 1935. *W. A. Camwell*

Pwhlleli on 16th August 1936 with Nos. 892, 2287 and inside 2572, 2465 and 2525.

W. A. Camwell

Rhymney shed, built originally by the Rhymney Railway, is seen in 1935. The locomotive nearest the camera is No. 77, an 0–6–2T of the ex-Rhymney Railway Class 'P1'.

L & GRP cty. David & Charles

READING

570	574	1240	1743	1880	2235	2242	2243	2253	2264
2305	2346	2358	2369	2404	2561	2570	2747	2784	2859
2868	2937	3005	3020	3025	3026	3286	3304	3323	3341
3356	3377	3382	3404	3434	3441	4384	4392	4827	4914
4938	4963	5339	5735	5914	5921	5924	6109	6110	6131
6132	6138	6140	6154	6318	6357	6373	6385	6623	7318
7708	7788	8740	8742	8766	9300	9302	9305	9317	9319

Steam Railmotor 37

RHYMNEY

34	39	42	46	76	77	79	80	81	83
136	141	5655	5660	5683	5690	5692	5696		

ROSS-ON-WYE

829 1455 1509

ST. BLAZEY

1223	1225	1227	1446	1587	1703	1736	1738	1792	1797
1819	1900	2740	2752	2755	2785	3590	4215	4508	4516
4517	4521	4548	4584	5516	5573	7715	7716		

ST. IVES

4406

ST. PHILIP'S MARSH, BRISTOL

869	907	986	1472	1498	1758	1789	1835	1902	1944
1945	1964	1967	1980	2007	2014	2015	2017	2031	2059
2126	2252	2260	2268	2269	2311	2317	2340	2347	2351
2373	2426	2437	2461	2467	2472	2473	2535	2552	2567
2632	2675	2678	2786	2814	2834	2839	2845	2848	3035
3045	3413	4055	4200	4309	4310	4348	4354	4374	4377
4379	4380	4387	4941	4945	4946	4970	4972	5110	5118
5123	5169	5716	5770	5771	5774	5781	5784	5785	5906
5917	5918	5929	6306	6333	6375	6390	6395	6600	6673
6710	6716	7306	7718	7719	7729	7735	7762	7782	7783
7784	7790	7792	7794	7795	8350	8351	8358	8703	8713
8714	8730	8733	8746	8747					

Steam Railmotors 76 77 81

SALISBURY

2047 2357 2820 2836 2870 3306 3391 3431 7307 8329

SEVERN TUNNEL JUNCTION

1557	1708	1714	1847	1875	2480	2521	2562	2603	2614
2624	2644	2659	2664	2669	2802	2822	2823	2824	2826
2831	2835	2852	2853	2876	3012	3013	3016	3154	3157
3159	3165	3167	3169	3172	3174	3175	3176	3177	3178
3179	3182	3188	3189	3439	4355	5306	5625	5626	5787
6349	6639	6691	7304	8326	8710	8716			

SHREWSBURY

1041	1045	1075	1507	1949	1965	1968	2004	2006	2010
2089	2322	2348	2419	2425	2442	2460	2462	2475	2477
2928	3008	3273	3373	3374	3383	3414	3562	3563	3569
4021	4025	4031	4041	4046	4051	4058	4064	4068	4332
4362	5397	6320	6342	6399	6602	6625	7317	7796	

SLOUGH

2046	2069	2074	2087	2112	3564	3919	6100	6104	6113
6114	6116	6118	6119	6120	6121	6123	6124	6129	6130
6136	6142	6145	6146	6149	6150	6152	6155	6157	6158
7731									

SOUTHALL

1152	1548	1716	1765	1767	1836	1850	1877	1996	2072
2376	2489	2765	2787	2843	2854	3408	3565	3596	4589
4826	5400	5401	5408	5409	5410	5412	5413	5415	5416
5417	5418	5500	5744	6107	6112	6128	6133	6139	6147
6148	6153	6156	6159	8757	8758	9316			

Diesel Railcar 1
Steam Railmotors 30 91 92

STAFFORD ROAD

92	1047	1442	1536	1547	1558	1567	1632	1749	1766
1771	1809	1869	1892	1951	2030	2061	2383	2386	2413
2414	2423	2488	2704	2914	2924	2929	2945	3021	3276
3358	3381	3571	4029	4034	4062	4065	4066	4089	4096
4097	4338	4373	4393	4917	4924	5130	5148	5153	5164

Swansea East Dock shed in 1935.

L & GRP, courtesy David & Charles

5174 5312 5323 5330 5377 5404 5934 5935 5938 5940
6005 6006 6008 6014 6019 6311 6403 6744 7315 7705
8307 8363

STAFFORD ROAD WORKS

 517 772 1506 1508 1519 1744 1750 1782 1784 1812
2028 2096 2106 2256 2257 2388 2444 2525 2550 3252
3277 4596 5119 5149 5150 5173 5177 5505 7706 8393

STAINES
4825

STOURBRIDGE
1094 1518 1522 1523 1527 1528 1541 1748 1777 1803
1863 2102 2104 2105 2107 2108 2109 2110 2152 2158
2320 2359 2378 2469 2438 2569 2604 2615 2621 2655
2703 2708 2710 2718 2719 2758 2791 3321 4511 4527
5102 5105 5112 5113 5116 5120 5122 5125 5128 5131
5135 5137 5140 5142 5145 5152 5156 5156 5182 5188
5532 5790 5791 5794 5795 6404 6405 6721 6748 8725
Steam Railmotors   64   66   93

STRATFORD-ON-AVON
3281 3423 3426 5108 5134 5139 5154

SWANSEA EAST DOCK
 359 408 696 701 779 929 935 942 943 968
 974 1098 1104 1629 1709 1710 1828 2134 2139 2166
2652 2663 2666 2789 4209 4210 4250 4255 4272 5214
5221 5229 5231 5232 5235 5253 5262 5269 5272 5688
5704 5705 5743 6677 6684 6713 6714 6715 7755 7785

SWINDON
 217 571 835 868 1007 1008 1011 1013 1119 1121
1124 1395 1396 1398 1399 1426 1433 1436 1477 1494
1497 1660 1731 2044 2119 2456 2528 2534 2564 2620
2677 2803 2827 2851 2903 2906 2913 2932 2935 2938
2939 2942 2943 2946 2954 2955 2981 3017 3019 3046
3340 3364 3375 4022 4563 4592 4906 4973 5355 5356
5567 5801 5802 5805 5806 5911 6347 6363 6711 6724
6733 6734 6735 6736 6737 6738 6739 6740 6741 7300
7728 8301 8354 8357 8702 8741

SWINDON WORKS
 892 905 987 1155 1336 1466 1570 1646 1650 1881
1908 2079 2114 2115 2255 2301 2403 2471 2512 2578
2626 2629 2636 2662 2748 2771 2774 2833 2840 2861
2941 2952 3007 3014 3223 3259 3266 3366 3410 3438
4014 4048 4063 4072 4079 4086 4090 4092 4095 4230
4244 4252 4263 4328 4350 4381 4383 4398 4510 4513
4526 4528 4540 4550 4565 4916 4919 4937 4958 4975
4986 4994 5002 5022 5126 5178 5187 5319 5396 5406
5414 5502 5507 5510 5522 5528 5547 5673 5760 6011
6018 6026 6101 6111 6115 6326 6378 6406 6634 7308
7778 7779 7789 7791 7799 8325 8364 8700 8711 8727
8743
Steam Railmotor   71

SWINDON STOCK SHED
1746 1764 1794 1976 2393 2989 3022 3582 4060 4221
4298 4928 5005 5132 5317 5803 5902 6017 6105 6354
6676 7798 8333 8765
Steam Railmotors   72   75   79   98

SWINDON F. POOL
1599 1793 1921 2251 2486 2541 2634 2772 2873 2883
2953 2976 2979 3291 3362 3363 3412 3598 4001 4044
4069 4364 4559 4930 6361 7700 8729 9301
Steam Railmotors   55   65   88   97

TAUNTON
854 1573 1760 1899 1925 1956 1993 2261 2265 2266
2267 2410 2416 2482 2517 2527 2911 2912 2920 2934
2987 3186 3187 3331 3453 4304 4313 4321 4531 4537
4569 4571 4581 5127 5172 5503 5521 5537 5542 5543
5571 6309

TETBURY
1440

TIVERTON JUNCTION
4808 5812

TONDU
1171 1174 1296 1561 1577 1725 1856 1870 1886 2130
2701 2727 2729 2735 2745 2761 3347 4227 4232 4262
4403 4408 5202 5707 5708 5709 5776 5792 5797 7712
7720 7721 7725 7736 7748

TRAWSFYNYDD
1780

TREHERBERT
152   279   365   366   368   373   378   399   409   486
792   793   794   5601 5608 5611 5615 5627 5636 5639
5640 5646 5659 5665 5676 5680 5687 5691 5695 5698

TRURO
1463 1464 1499 1799 1815 1840 2725 2776 3581 4500
4502 4503 4509 4525 4547 4959 4990 5569 8313 8362
8372 8381

TYSELEY
1501 1540 1549 1554 1742 1763 1770 1786 1788 1790
1824 1950 1955 2036 2052 2078 2092 2145 2439 2575
2712 2714 2744 2753 2815 2837 2874 2875 2878 2926
2927 2930 3158 3190 3274 3360 3369 3403 3417 3450
4307 4329 4333 4336 4343 4375 4386 4501 4579 4580
4700 4701 4943 4952 5100 5103 5104 5106 5117 5138
5141 5143 5151 5157 5162 5163 5165 5170 5175 5180
5181 5186 5321 5519 5724 5725 5726 5738 5742 6368
6372 6377 6396 6745 6746 6747 7301 7320 7714 7758
7797 8300 8726

TYSELEY WORKS
2262 3001

WALLINGFORD
542

WATLINGTON
2081

WELLINGTON
768 1514 1524 1787 2706 2716 2717 2720 3210 3216
3222 3309 5129 5810

WELLS
2400 5564

St. Blazey loco shed in 1936, with an '850' class pannier tank in the foreground and a '2721' class pannier on the far side. Two unidentified '45XX' small Prairies can be seen in the shed on the roads adjacent to the '2721' class tank.   *Photomatic*

WELSHPOOL
855

WELSHPOOL (Narrow Gauge)
822   823

WESTBURY
1644 1816 1915 2364 2394 2435 2518 2529 2566 2639
2779 2780 2933 2977 3283 3316 3343 3354 3384 3389
3421 4314 4315 4326 4349 4365 4368 4829 4932 4964
4982 5419 5511 5546 5556 5570 5689 5718 6341 6382
6384 6690 6712 7302 7711 7726 7727 7730 7749 8722
8744

WESTON-SUPER-MARE
2537 2915 3335 5535 6314

WEYMOUTH
 219 833 1163 1281 1331 1465 1566 1831 1841 2194
2195 3330 3345 3432 4370 4923 4929 4947 4992 5367
5919 6307 6344 6397 7309 8320 8391

WHITCHURCH
2565

WHITLAND
1623 1910 1911 1983 1994 2409 2432 2476 2544 4505
4506 4514 4515 5539 5568

WINCHESTER
2547

WORCESTER
 464 1220 1246 1853 1961 1989 2001 2016 2019 2101
2121 2263 2310 2325 2328 2350 2380 2431 2458 2481
2485 2515 2551 2557 2568 2577 2613 2743 2757 2783
3027 3348 3353 3368 3371 3394 3406 3418 3428 3449
4013 4033 4038 4049 4067 4305 4308 4312 4327 4359
4558 4594 4804 4818 4996 5124 5303 5375 5527 5808
5817 6319 6353 6358 6370 8717

YATTON
5529 5800

YEOVIL
1166 1179 1180 1525 1598 1620 1624 1860 5548 5554

Weston Super Mare on 22nd August 1937 with Nos. 2955, 2564, 4031, 5962, 2954, 4071, 4041, 6811, and LMS Nos. 1002, 5525, 4273 and 4561.

W. A. Camwell

APPENDIX A

DIVISIONAL LOCO SHED ORGANISATION AT 1st JANUARY 1934

The list of locomotive allocations by shed has been given in alphabetical order for ease of reference. The locomotive sheds were actually administered as nine divisions covering separate geographical areas. Within each division there were several major sheds, many of which had smaller sub-sheds. Locomotives from the sub-sheds would go to their parent shed for routine maintenance or minor running repairs.

The divisional organisation of sheds listed here is taken from the official 1934 allocation register. However, it will be noted that this list presents certain minor inconsistencies, when compared with the allocations themselves, while there are other points of interest as follows:-

(i) Cleobury Mortimer is listed as a sub-shed of Kidderminster, but no locomotives were allocated there —

28 and 29 which worked at Cleobury Mortimer were recorded as being allocated to Kidderminster.

(ii) Kingham is not listed as a sub-shed (of Worcester), but loco 1004 is recorded as being allocated there.

(iii) Coke Ovens shed was officially closed on 7th December 1933, but locos were still recorded as being allocated there until early 1934.

(iv) Merthyr shed was transferred to Cardiff Valleys division on 26th September 1934.

(v) Penmaenpool is listed as a sub-shed of Chester, but it is usually listed as a sub-shed of Croes Newydd.

(vi) Tetbury and Cirencester were sub-sheds of Gloucester, but their locos were supplied from Swindon.

DIVISIONAL ORGANISATION (Sub-sheds inset)

LONDON DIVISION
Old Oak Common
Southall
  Staines
Slough
  Aylesbury
  Marlow
  Watlington
Reading
  Basingstoke
  Henley
Oxford
  Fairford
  Abingdon
Didcot
  Lambourn
  Wallingford
  Newbury
  Winchester

BRISTOL DIVISION
Swindon
  Swindon Works
  Swindon F. Pool
  Swindon Stock
  Andover Junction
  Chippenham
  Malmesbury
Bath Road, Bristol
  Bath
  Wells
  Weston-Super-Mare
  St. Philip's Marsh
  Yatton
Westbury
  Frome
  Salisbury
Yeovil
Weymouth
  Bridport

NEWTON ABBOT DIVISION
Taunton
  Barnstaple
  Bridgwater
  Minehead
Exeter
  Tiverton Junction
Newton Abbot
  Ashburton
  Kingsbridge
  Moretonhampstead
Laira
  Launceston
  Plymouth
  Princetown
St. Blazey
  Bodmin
  Moorswater
Truro
Penzance
  Helston
  St. Ives

WOLVERHAMPTON DIVISION
Birkenhead
Chester
  Penmaenpool
Croes Newydd
  Bala
  Trawsfynydd
Shrewsbury
  Ludlow
Wellington
  Crewe
  Much Wenlock
Stafford Road, Wolverhampton
  Oxley, Wolverhampton
Stourbridge
Tyseley
  Alcester
  Stratford-on-Avon
Leamington
Banbury

WORCESTER DIVISION
Worcester
  Evesham
  Honeybourne
  Kingham *see (ii)*
Hereford
  Kington
  Ledbury
  Leominster
  Ross-on-Wye
Kidderminster
  Cleobury Mortimer *see (i)*
Gloucester
  Brimscombe
  Chalford
  Cheltenham (Malvern Rd.)
  Cheltenham (High St.)
  Lydney
  Cirencester
  Tetbury

NEWPORT DIVISION
Severn Tunnel Junction
Ebbw Junction, Newport
Aberbeeg
Pill, Newport
Cardiff Canton
Llantrisant
Tondu
  Bridgend
  Aberdare
Pontypool Road
  Branches Fork
  Pontrilas
Merthyr *see (iv)*

NEATH DIVISION
Duffryn, Port Talbot
Neath
  Glyn Neath
  Neath and Brecon
Swansea East Dock
Danygraig

Landore
Llanelly
  Burry Port
  Llanelly & Mynydd Mawr
  Llandovery
  Pantyffynnon
Carmarthen
  Newcastle Emlyn
Neyland
  Cardigan
  Milford Haven
  Pembroke Dock
  Whitland
Goodwick, Fishguard

CARDIFF VALLEYS DIVISION
Cathays, Cardiff
  Radyr Junction
Treherbert
  Ferndale
Abercynon
  Coke Ovens *see (iii)*
Barry
Cardiff East Dock
Cae Harris, Dowlais
  Dowlais Central
Rhymney

CENTRAL WALES DIVISION
Oswestry
  Llanfyllin
  Llanidloes
  Moat Lane
  Welshpool
  Welshpool (Narrow Gauge)
  Whitchurch
Machynlleth
  Aberayron
Aberystwyth
  Aberystwyth (Narrow Gauge)
Portmadoc
  Pwllheli
  Corris (Narrow Gauge)
Brecon
  Builth Wells

APPENDIX B

LOCOMOTIVES IN STORE ON 1st JANUARY 1934

In the early 1930s the South Wales coal industry was in recession, and consequently demands for locomotive power were reduced. As a result, locomotives were placed into store at Swindon Stock Shed and several South Wales sheds. One of these locations was at Caerphilly, where the carriage shed was used.

The number of locomotives in store on 1st January 1934 was 74, and these are listed separately in the front of the 1934 allocation register, in addition to being shown as 'stored' in the normal part of the register. In one case, different locations are given; 0—4—0 dock tank 1338 is shown as being at Cardiff East Dock in the stored locos list and at Cathays in the allocation register.

The stored locos include 2—8—0 tanks 5275-5294, which were during 1934 converted to 2—8—2 tanks 7200-7219, for hauling longer range coal trains.

The locos stored on 1st January 1934 were:-

CATHAYS, CARDIFF

60	61	62	63	64	65	68	69	70	71
73	75	281	285	315	333	711	713	720	722
754									

CARDIFF EAST DOCK

1338

CAERPHILLY CARRIAGE SHED

4202 4214 4217 4218 4222 4237 4245 4267 4293 4295
5223 5280 5283 5284 5286 5290 5293 5662

NEWPORT EBBW JUNCTION

5281 5282 5285 5291

SWINDON STOCK SHED

4248 5227 5242 5264 5275 5276 5277 5278 5279 5287
5288 5289 5292 5294 5604 5612 5613 5628 5631 5632
5633 5634 5638 5645 5649 5656 5657 5663 5675 6674

APPENDIX C

LOCOMOTIVES WAITING TO ENTER WORKS AND WORKS PROCEDURE AT SWINDON

In addition to recording those locomotives receiving attention at the various works, as listed in the allocations by shed, the registers denote those engines which were at their home shed awaiting a visit to the works.

It is not possible to give a complete list for 1st January 1934 of locos which were awaiting a visit to the works, since this would require information from the last time period of the 1933 register which is unfortunately missing from the records at Kew. A complete list can, however, be given for the first four week period of 1934, ending on 13th January 1934. This is reproduced below.

The number of locomotives held awaiting attention appears rather high — perhaps twice as many as at other times during 1934.

LOCOMOTIVES WAITING TO ENTER WORKS ON 13th JANUARY 1934

WAITING TO ENTER SWINDON WORKS

216 470 504 533 559 574 723 762 772 806
813 837 872 905 943 967 983 1161 1171 1220
1281 1376 1442 1530 1558 1587 1638 1706 1710 1747
1771 1796 1837 1839 1840 1846 1887 1896 1902 1967
1985 1993 2018 2026 2030 2042 2076 2078 2093 2098
2132 2152 2197 2235 2246 2250 2254 2264 2320 2322
2351 2404 2428 2435 2473 2476 2513 2527 2529 2532
2537 2548 2580 2608 2617 2622 2627 2637 2638 2641
2643 2646 2666 2676 2701 2719 2728 2764 2784 2795
2846 2852 2875 2878 2880 2945 3004 3010 3019 3032
3258 3290 3307 3318 3328 3331 3376 3391 3395 3406
3409 3423 3428 3429 3437 3439 3442 3557 3567 3591
3627 4034 4051 4210 4273 4282 4301 4332 4334 4341
4347 4356 4372 4380 4394 4399 4502 4503 4517 4576
4943 4948 4954 5011 5131 5134 5150 5153 5182 5267
5375 5377 5401 5516 5545 5546 5615 5648 5736 5776
6103 6112 6126 6313 6324 6359 6364 6366 6379 6387
6393 6398 6609 6650 6656 6679 6684 7742 7755 8302
8343 8369 8373 8734 8744

WAITING TO ENTER STAFFORD ROAD WORKS
1766 1965 2320 2414 5113 5135 5159 6404 6405 6721

WAITING TO ENTER CAERPHILLY WORKS
6616 6658

WAITING TO ENTER NEWTON ABBOT WORKS
5573

WORKS PROCEDURE AT SWINDON

Many of the locomotives which passed through Swindon Works are also recorded in the allocation register as staying briefly at Swindon F. Pool (F. stands for Factory), and Swindon Stock Shed. This may be illustrated by the example of 517 Class 0—4—2 tank No. 216. This was listed as a Banbury engine on 1st January 1934 and at the end of the subsequent four week periods as follows:

Loco No.	Shed at 1/1/34	Four week period ending				
		13/1	10/2	10/3	7/4	5/5
216	Banbury	5 Wait, Swindon Works	6 Swindon F. Pool	15 Swindon Works	16 I Swindon Stock Shed	Oxford

Waiting at Banbury for transfer to Swindon Works — 5th January. Transferred from Banbury to Swindon Factory Pool — 6th February. Entered Swindon Works from Factory Pool — 15th February. Moved to Swindon Stock Shed after overhaul — 16th March. (I indicates loco had Intermediate overhaul). Allocated to Oxford shed for duties by 5th May.

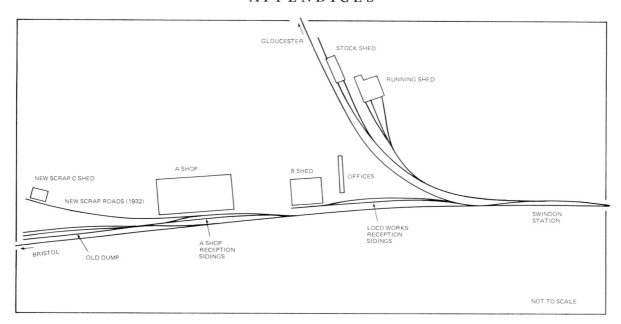

By the 1930s, the works dates of engines requiring routine attention tended to be programmed before the locomotives actually arrived at Swindon. It would seem that some were held at their home sheds for a period, awaiting the scheduled date — hence the regular entry 'Wait Swindon Works'. Such entries are made in the register in red ink, which is used throughout the Great Western allocation registers to indicate when a locomotive is not in running stock. Similar entries of 'Wt Stafford Rd Factory', 'Wt Newton Factory', 'Wt Caerphilly' are also used in the 1934 register.

Engines in running stock destined for Swindon Works were normally worked to Swindon Running Shed where they were taken out of traffic and subsequently sent the 400 yards over to the Works Reception Sidings. Here boilers were drained and tenders or bunkers emptied of coal. Tenders were detached and engines were shunted down to the reception sidings outside the 'A' shop. Tenders were held adjacent to the initial reception sidings, as they were repaired in the 'B' Shed, which was almost alongside. Some small engines were also repaired in the 'B' Shed, but they were always taken down to the 'A' Shop reception sidings and then called into 'B' Shed as required.

As soon as an engine had reached the initial Works Reception Sidings it was taken out of running stock (if this had not already been done) and was transferred to the Works jurisdiction. If the engine concerned was already programmed to enter the factory, it would only stay in the 'A' Shop Reception Sidings for about two days — just long enough for the inspectors (boiler, mechanical, etc.) to look over it to assess and detail the necessary repairs. Then the engine would be taken into the shops.

An alternative at the Works Reception Stage for locomotives not programmed to enter the works within a couple of days, or for those requiring repairs but not required for traffic, was for them to be put in the Swindon Factory Pool. This theoretically held a number of locomotives whose repair was not urgent. They could be called into the shops when there was capacity to deal with them. The Factory Pool had been created due to the slump in traffic of the late 1920s/early 1930s. During this period there were large numbers of locomotives around Swindon Works which were not immediately programmed for overhaul and not urgently required for traffic.

By 1934 the designation 'Swindon F. Pool' appears to have been more widely used, to represent those locomotives which had a significant wait between arriving at the Works Reception Sidings and entering the shops. In the example given above, it would seem that No. 216 arrived at Swindon on 6th February 1934, and entered the shops on 15th February. It was not just the smaller or older engines which are recorded as waiting in the 'F. Pool' before entering the works in 1934. For example, a total of 15 members of the 93XX class passed through Swindon Works during 1934, and nine of these are recorded as having spent a period in the 'F. Pool' first.

Locomotives in the 'F. Pool' were under works jurisdiction, but not necessarily to be found in any specified siding. They could remain in the 'A' Shop Reception Sidings, or perhaps start there and subsequently be moved by the works shunter in order to get to an engine which was wanted in the works. An alternative was the Old Dump sidings, just past the 'A' Shop, which had been released by the addition of the New Scrap Roads and 'C' Scrap Shop in 1932.

After completion of repairs, many locomotives were already programmed to return either to their former shed or on to another. Some, however, when ready to return to running stock, were not immediately required. Such locomotives, including newly constructed engines, were put in (or around) the Swindon Stock Shed. For example, four of the fifteen 93XX engines repaired at Swindon during 1934 moved afterwards to Swindon Stock Shed; each of these is recorded there for just one four-week period, before being forwarded to a running shed.

APPENDIX D

INITIAL ALLOCATIONS OF LOCOS WHICH ENTERED SERVICE DURING 1934

The shed to which each new locomotive or railcar entering service during 1934 was first allocated is detailed in this appendix. Sometimes this initial allocation was only of short duration, with the loco soon being transferred, often within the same division.

0–6–0PT '1366' CLASS

1366	Swindon
1367	Swindon
1368	Swindon
1369	Swindon
1370	Swindon

0–6–0 '2251' CLASS

2271	St. Philip's Marsh
2272	Carmarthen
2273	Carmarthen
2274	Worcester
2275	Stourbridge
2276	Reading
2277	St. Philip's Marsh
2278	Worcester
2279	Oxley
2280	Didcot

0–4–2T '4800' CLASS

4830	Aylesbury
4831	Ebbw Junction
4832	Tiverton Junction
4833	Swindon
4834	Penmaenpool
4835	St. Blazey
4836	Swindon
4837	Aberayron
4838	Reading
4839	Neath

4–6–0 '4073' CASTLE CLASS

5023	Old Oak Common
5024	Taunton
5025	Old Oak Common
5026	Newton Abbot
5027	Old Oak Common
5028	Laira
5029	Old Oak Common
5030	Exeter
5031	Stafford Road
5032	Shrewsbury

2–6–2T '5101' CLASS

5190	Tyseley
5191	Stafford Road
5192	Leamington
5193	Stourbridge
5194	Tyseley
5195	Banbury
5196	Stourbridge
5197	Stourbridge
5198	Stafford Road
5199	Tyseley

0–6–0PT '5700' CLASS

8770	Old Oak Common
8771	Old Oak Common
8772	Old Oak Common
8773	Old Oak Common
8774	Southall
8775	Neath
8776	Pontypool Road
8777	Ebbw Junction
8778	Tondu
8779	Westbury
8780	Landore
8781	Llanelly
8782	Neath
8783	St. Blazey
8784	Tyseley
8785	Landore
8786	Ebbw Junction
8787	Stourbridge
8788	Aberbeeg
8789	Landore
8790	St. Philip's Marsh
8791	Stourbridge
8792	Stafford Road
8793	St. Philip's Marsh
8794	Ebbw Junction
8795	Bath
8796	Llantrisant
8797	Tyseley
8798	Oxley
8799	Aberdare
9700	Old Oak Common
9711	Laira
9712	Ebbw Junction
9713	Severn Tunnel Junction
9714	Stafford Road
9715	Shrewsbury
9716	Taunton
9717	Newton Abbot
9718	Exeter
9719	Stafford Road
9720	Yeovil
9721	St. Philip's Marsh
9722	Oxford
9723	Aberbeeg
9724	Tyseley
9725	Old Oak Common
9726	Old Oak Common
9727	Stafford Road
9728	Stourbridge
9729	St. Philip's Marsh

0–6–0PT '6400' CLASS

6410	Aberdare
6411	Cathays
6412	Landore
6413	Cardiff Canton
6414	Laira
6415	Ebbw Junction
6416	Llantrisant
6417	Laira
6418	Stourbridge
6419	Laira

2–8–2T '7200' CLASS

7200	Llanelly
7201	Llanelly
7202	Ebbw Junction
7203	Ebbw Junction
7204	Cardiff Canton
7205	Aberdare
7206	Llanelly
7207	Severn Tunnel Junction
7208	Severn Tunnel Junction
7209	Severn Tunnel Junction
7210	Severn Tunnel Junction
7211	Ebbw Junction
7212	Ebbw Junction
7213	Cardiff Canton
7214	Swansea East Dock
7215	Pantyffynnon
7216	Swindon
7217	Ebbw Junction
7218	Swindon
7219	Cardiff Canton

DIESEL RAILCARS

2	Tyseley
3	Cardiff
4	Tyseley
5	Oxford
6	Worcester

APPENDIX E

ALLOCATION OF TENDERS TO LOCOMOTIVES

Recording of Tenders in the Allocation Register

In addition to giving the shed allocation of each locomotive throughout the thirteen 4-week periods of the year, the 1934 allocations register also records which tender was paired with each engine. The tender numbers are marked in the register in pencil (all other entries are in ink), adjacent to the locomotive number, evidently so that these details could be updated throughout the year. When a loco entered the works for an overhaul, it would lose the tender it had been paired with and would often collect another after its overhaul. One consequence of this is that the tender allocations given in the 1934 register therefore reflect the situation at the end of 1934, rather than the beginning. Hence all locomotives constructed up to the end of 1934 are listed in this appendix.

Where locomotives were condemned during 1934, or were in the works at the end of 1934, the tender entry in the register has been rubbed out. In some cases it had been possible to detect the number which has been erased and such entries are given here in brackets (e.g. tender (1257) for loco 1195). In these cases the tender given was therefore the last one hauled by the loco prior to withdrawal or shopping. Where it has not been possible to read with certainty the rubbed out tender number, the relevant tender number has been found from the locomotive history sheets, which are also held in the Public Record Office. A few locos scrapped early in 1934 were never paired with a tender during that year, for example, Dean Goods 2301, which was condemned on 5th January 1934; in these cases the last tender paired with the locomotive is recorded here.

It follows that a few tenders are shown more than once in this register. For example, tender No. 1434, which was paired with locomotive No. 2454 at the end of 1934, is also recorded as the last tender paired with locomotive No. 354, of the Beyer Goods class.

List of Tender Types

Great Western Railway tenders were numbered in a special series, from 1, which eventually reached 4126. The various construction lots were issued diagram numbers in the series A1 to A192. The series had reached A136 by the end of 1934. A complete history of the various diagrams, with construction dates, is given in Part 12 of the RCTS history, 'The Locomotives of the Great Western Railway'. Summary information, detailing the various types of Great Western tender extant at 1934, and the relevant number series, is given below:-

3000 Gallons, 7 ft 6 in x 7 ft 6 in wheelbase, built 1884-1906.
Diagrams	A5/10-12/14/15/17-21/31/32/45/47-50/52/54/57/ 61-4/71
Numbers	852/904-1077/1219-1258/1309-1314/1436-1455/ 1462-1508/1519-1538/1540-1559/1562-1571/ 1587-1631/1685-1694

2500 Gallons, 6 ft 6 in x 6 ft 6 in wheelbase, built 1884-1903.
Diagrams	A6/7/9/22/23/26/29/30/33/35/37-39/41-44/58
Numbers	103/111-114/117-120/122/853-892/894-903/ 1078-1117/1138-1157/1179-1218/1259-1288/ 1315-1345/1366-1435/1572-1581

2000 Gallons, 5 ft 6 in x 5 ft 6 in wheelbase, built 1895-1899.
Diagrams	A24/25/27/34
Numbers	1118-1137/1158-1177/1289-1308

2600 Gallons, 6 ft 6 in x 6 ft 6 in wheelbase, built 1896.
Diagram	A28
Number	1178

2400 Gallons, 5 ft 6 in x 5 ft 6 in wheelbase, built 1900-1901.
Diagram	A40
Numbers	1346-1365

4000 Gallons, 7 ft 6 in x 7 ft 6 in wheelbase, built 1900-1904.
Diagrams	A46/51/53/55/56/60
Numbers	1456-1461/1509-1518/1539/1560/1561/1582

3500 Gallons, 7 ft 6 in x 7 ft 6 in wheelbase, built 1905-1926.
Diagrams	A65-70/72-75/77-104/106-112
Numbers	1632-1684/1695-1754/1756-2181/2202-2241/ 2312-2363/2366-2383

3500 Gallons, 5 ft 9 in x 5 ft 6 in x 5 ft 9 in bogie, built 1908.
Diagram	A76
Number	1755 (originally built to run with 'The Great Bear')

3500 Gallons, 7 ft 6 in x 7 ft 6 in wheelbase, built 1929-1930.
Diagram	A118
Numbers	2242-2268

4000 Gallons, 7 ft 6 in x 7 ft 6 in wheelbase, built 1926-1934.
Diagrams	A113/117/120/121/123/124/127/128/131/136
Numbers	2384-2449/2530-2656

*2586 was built with eight rigid wheels, 5 ft x 5 ft x 5 ft wheelbase.

ABSORBED TENDERS

Cambrian Railways

Ex-Cambrian Railway tenders were allocated GWR tender numbers 385-422, but in 1934 several still bore their Cambrian Railways numbers. Some were never renumbered.

The Cambrian numbers corresponding to the new GWR numbers were, in order:

18/20/31/48/80/99/101/77/19/32/74/76/85/95/GW 188/54/28/ 40/21/41/61/38/86/94/100/97/63/98/93/87/79/78/16/29/42/15/ 102/88.

*GW 188 was the tender which accompanied former GW loco 212.

NOTE: The above list is as shown in *The Locomotives of the Great Western Railway Part 11* (RCTS). Two additional ex-Cambrian Railways tenders are listed in the Great Western Railway Tender Register, 1931, which is held at the Public Record Office. These are Cambrian numbers 4 and 75. No corresponding Great Western numbers are given in the register for these two tenders. It will be noted that these tenders were still extant in 1934, being paired with locomotives No. 910 and 875 respectively.

Midland and South Western Railway

Ex-M & SWJR tenders were allocated GWR tender numbers 36/
43/44/62/92/95/540-546/548-555/557/558

Ex-R.O.D. Tenders

4000 Gallons, 6 ft 6 in x 6 ft 6 in wheelbase, built 1919.
Diagram   A105/114/115
Numbers   2181-2201/2450-2529

TENDER ALLOCATIONS

Locomotive number on left, Tender number on right

0-6-0 CAMBRIAN RAILWAYS '15' CLASS

844 — 42	873 — 391	894 — 409
849 — 15	887 — 410	895 — 412
855 — 408	892 — 398	896 — 406
864 — 29	893 — 102	

0-6-0 CAMBRIAN RAILWAYS '73' CLASS

875 — 75	880 — 415	885 — 88
876 — 396	882 — 395	
878 — 387	884 — 416	

0-6-0 CAMBRIAN RAILWAYS SMALL GOODS CLASS

898 — 386	908 — 1622
900 — 16	910 — 4

0-6-0 MIDLAND & SOUTH WESTERN RAILWAY

1003 — 553	1007 — 544	1011 — 546
1004 — 550	1008 — 545	1013 — 557
1005 — 543	1009 — 552	
1006 —(551)	1010 —(554)	

4-4-0 MIDLAND & SOUTH WESTERN RAILWAY

1119 — 540	1123 — 541	1128 — 542
1121 — 36	1124 — 549	
1122 — 43	1126 — 548	

2-4-0 MIDLAND & SOUTH WESTERN RAILWAY

1334 — 92
1335 — 62
1336 — 44

0-6-0 '322' BEYER CLASS

354 —(1434)

0-6-0 '388' STANDARD (ARMSTRONG) GOODS CLASS

1094 —(1331)
1195 —(1257)

0-6-0 '2251' COLLETT CLASS

2251 — 983	2261 — 1437	2271 — 1042
2252 — 1546	2262 — 1602	2272 — 1550
2253 — 1505	2263 — 929	2273 — 1454
2254 — 1495	2264 — 1444	2274 — 1076
2255 — 1692	2265 — 1470	2275 — 1520
2256 — 1244	2266 — 1567	2276 — 1478
2257 — 1548	2267 — 1563	2277 — 1535
2258 — 1591	2268 — 1590	2278 — 1532
2259 — 1066	2269 — 1451	2279 — 1691
2260 — 1235	2270 — 973	2280 — 1690

0-6-0 '2301' DEAN GOODS CLASS

2301 — (949)	2411 — 1462	2481 — 1551
2303 — 1557	2412 — 1003	2482 — 1185
2305 — 1504	2413 — 993	2483 — 954
2310 —(1323)	2414 — 1183	2484 — 1607
2311 —(1425)	2415 — 1262	2485 — 904
2313 — 1239	2416 — 1333	2486 — 1237
2315 — 1117	2417 — 1530	2487 — 1378
2316 — (878)	2418 — 1538	2488 — 1008
2317 —(1624)	2419 — 1015	2489 — 1402
2320 — 1055	2421 — 1049	2490 — 1600
2321 — 1038	2422 — 1373	2511 — 915
2322 — 930	2423 — 852	2512 — 912
2323 — 928	2424 — 996	2513 — 943
2325 — 1594	2425 — 1011	2514 — 1020
2327 — 1191	2426 — 1057	2515 — 1113
2328 — 967	2427 — 1324	2516 — 961
2332 — 1534	2428 — 948	2517 — 1605
2336 — (978)	2429 — 1282	2518 — 991
2337 — 1531	2430 — 1343	2519 — 1522
2339 — 1405	2431 — 965	2520 — 1429
2340 — 981	2432 — 939	2521 — 1276
2341 —(1208)	2433 — 941	2522 — 1043
2342 — 1483	2434 — 1122	2523 — 932
2343 — 1039	2435 — 944	2524 — 1583
2345 — 1085	2436 — 1056	2525 — 118
2346 — 972	2437 — 1688	2526 — 1570
2347 — 1041	2438 — 1031	2527 — 1089
2348 — 1000	2439 — 1024	2528 — 1630
2349 — 1230	2440 — 1252	2529 — 1313
2350 — 902	2441 — 1157	2530 — 1430
2351 — 960	2442 — 976	2531 — 953
2352 — 1466	2443 — 1423	2532 — 1596
2353 — 117	2444 — 982	2533 — 1328
2354 — 1628	2445 — 1595	2534 — 1565
2356 — 979	2446 — 1617	2535 — 1449
2357 — 1629	2447 — 1686	2536 — 1014
2358 — (918)	2449 — 1006	2537 — 1524
2359 — 1059	2450 — 1357	2538 — 908
2360 — 1416	2451 — 1224	2539 — 1242
2381 — 1571	2452 — 900	2540 — 112
2382 — 969	2454 — 1434	2541 — 1010
2383 — 1037	2455 — 1500	2543 — 1559
2384 — 1606	2456 — 1608	2544 — 1275
2385 — 1104	2457 — 1199	2545 — 1254
2386 — 1073	2458 — 1330	2546 — 1257
2388 — 1542	2459 — 1322	2547 — 1693
2389 — 855	2460 — 1070	2548 — 1321
2390 — 1589	2461 — 999	2549 — 1236
2392 — 1009	2462 — 1074	2550 — 1034
2393 — 1036	2463 — 1022	2551 — 950
2394 — 1246	2464 — 1058	2552 — 1312
2395 — 1497	2465 — 1149	2553 — 974
2396 —(1190)	2466 — 1552	2554 — 1214
2397 — 1498	2467 — 1420	2555 — 1101
2398 — 1139	2468 — 1030	2556 — 1255
2399 — 1623	2469 — 1203	2557 — 931
2400 — 1310	2470 — 1613	2558 — 987
2401 — 1540	2471 — 910	2559 — 977
2402 — 1202	2472 — 1393	2560 — 1579
2403 — 1598	2473 — 917	2561 — 963
2404 — 1241	2474 — 1541	2562 — 1053
2405 — 1245	2475 — 1054	2564 — 1544
2406 — 1472	2476 — 1013	2565 — 927
2407 — 992	2477 — 1447	2566 — 970
2408 — 1273	2478 — 1443	2567 — 1338
2409 — 938	2479 — 1341	2568 — 1225
2410 — 1453	2480 — 985	2569 — 1326

2570 — 1097	2574 — 1018	2578 — 1508
2571 — 1406	2575 — 1048	2579 — 1178
2572 — 1441	2576 — 1362	2580 — 1564
2573 — 1562	2577 — 1381	

0–6–0 '2361' CLASS

2362 — 1499	2370 — 1232	2376 — 1329
2364 — (1000)	2372 — 1063	2378 — 1061
2368 — 1575	2373 — (962)	2380 — 1078
2369 — 884	2375 — 1573	

2–6–0 '2600' ABERDARE CLASS

2600 — 2490	2627 — (2525)	2654 — 1558
2601 — 2529	2628 — 1456	2655 — 2488
2602 — (2491)	2629 — 1460	2656 — 2510
2603 — 2452	2630 — (1471)	2657 — 1599
2604 — 1549	2631 — 1489	2658 — (1510)
2605 — 2502	2632 — 1587	2659 — 1228
2606 — 2492	2633 — 1523	2660 — 2505
2607 — (2501)	2634 — 2483	2661 — 2486
2608 — 2187	2635 — 2487	2662 — 998
2609 — (1535)	2636 — 2513	2663 — 2504
2610 — 2183	2637 — 2527	2664 — 2517
2611 — (2483)	2638 — 2484	2665 — 2521
2612 — 1440	2639 — 1458	2666 — (2505)
2613 — 2496	2640 — 2516	2667 — 1536
2614 — 2201	2641 — (1042)	2668 — 2511
2615 — 1481	2642 — 1492	2669 — 2491
2616 — 1512	2643 — 2520	2670 — 2498
2617 — (1566)	2644 — 2199	2671 — 2506
2618 — 2481	2645 — 913	2672 — 1032
2619 — 2515	2646 — 1537	2673 — 2522
2620 — 2493	2647 — 966	2674 — 2526
2621 — (2506)	2648 — 1516	2675 — 1464
2622 — 2523	2649 — 2512	2676 — 1492
2623 — 1510	2650 — 1529	2677 — 2494
2624 — 1547	2651 — 1450	2678 — 2507
2625 — 2509	2652 — 1243	2679 — 1586
2626 — 2514	2653 — 2518	2680 — 2528

2–8–0 '2800' CLASS

2800 — 2005	2826 — 1668	2852 — 2083
2801 — 1780	2827 — 1912	2853 — 2343
2802 — 2336	2828 — 2218	2854 — 2090
2803 — 1830	2829 — 2128	2855 — 2066
2804 — 2170	2830 — 2028	2856 — 2060
2805 — 1905	2831 — 1702	2857 — 1903
2806 — 1974	2832 — 2237	2858 — 1769
2807 — 1879	2833 — 1796	2859 — 2104
2808 — 1855	2834 — 2140	2860 — 1847
2809 — 2205	2835 — 1680	2861 — 1930
2810 — 2080	2836 — 1673	2862 — 2033
2811 — 2092	2837 — 1800	2863 — 2372
2812 — 1701	2838 — 1895	2864 — 1935
2813 — 1928	2839 — 2021	2865 — 1659
2814 — 1726	2840 — 1817	2866 — 2213
2815 — 2206	2841 — 2360	2867 — 1652
2816 — 1814	2842 — 1654	2868 — 1887
2817 — 1862	2843 — 1740	2869 — 1750
2818 — 2119	2844 — 2097	2870 — 1872
2819 — 2109	2845 — 1907	2871 — 1789
2820 — 2048	2846 — 2211	2872 — 2363
2821 — 1807	2847 — 1894	2873 — 2357
2822 — 2344	2848 — 2018	2874 — 1718
2823 — 1975	2849 — 2020	2875 — 2039
2824 — 2204	2850 — 2093	2876 — 2178
2825 — 1820	2851 — 2235	2877 — 2150

2878 — 2158	2880 — 1892	2882 — 2050
2879 — 1908	2881 — 2126	2883 — 2079

4–6–0 '2900' SAINT CLASS

2902 — 1795	2929 — 1851	2950 — 1513
2903 — 1838	2930 — 2233	2951 — 1926
2905 — 1906	2931 — 2257	2952 — 1939
2906 — 1827	2932 — 2231	2953 — 1854
2908 — 2147	2933 — 1662	2954 — 2124
2911 — 1793	2934 — 1511	2955 — 1778
2912 — 1945	2935 — 1561	2971 — 2096
2913 — 2353	2936 — 2330	2972 — 1938
2914 — 1774	2937 — 9094	2975 — 2215
2915 — 1772	2938 — 2244	2976 — (1761)
2916 — 1755	2939 — 1936	2977 — 1877
2917 — 1866	2940 — 2240	2978 — 1835
2918 — 1819	2941 — 1763	2979 — 1865
2920 — 1860	2942 — 1831	2980 — 2006
2921 — 2228	2943 — 2057	2981 — 1509
2922 — 1944	2944 — 2319	2982 — (2026)
2923 — (1514)	2945 — 1649	2983 — 1788
2924 — 2064	2946 — 1858	2987 — 2023
2926 — 2347	2947 — 1794	2988 — 2208
2927 — 1640	2948 — 2238	2989 — 1757
2928 — 2167	2949 — 2166	2990 — 1840

2–8–0 Ex-R.O.D.

3000 — 2455	3017 — 2182	3034 — 2189
3001 — 2489	3018 — 2200	3035 — 2465
3002 — 2192	3019 — 2185	3036 — 2466
3003 — 2508	3020 — 2450	3037 — 2467
3004 — 2186	3021 — 2451	3038 — 2468
3005 — 2462	3022 — 2482	3039 — 2469
3006 — 2474	3023 — 2453	3040 — 2470
3007 — 2184	3024 — 2454	3041 — 2476
3008 — 2190	3025 — 2495	3042 — 2472
3009 — 2191	3026 — 2456	3043 — 2473
3010 — 2477	3027 — 2457	3044 — 2193
3011 — 2188	3028 — 2458	3045 — 2475
3012 — 2194	3029 — 2459	3046 — 2480
3013 — 2464	3030 — 2460	3047 — 2195
3014 — 2196	3031 — 2461	3048 — 2471
3015 — 2501	3032 — 2197	3049 — 2479
3016 — 2198	3033 — 2463	

2–4–0 '3206' BARNUM CLASS

3206 — (1041)	3216 — 1553	3223 — 1106
3210 — 1581	3217 — 1238	3225 — 1385
3211 — 1572	3219 — 1146	
3213 — 1248	3222 — 1345	

4–4–0 '3252' DUKE CLASS

3252 — 925	3266 — 956	3280 — 1369
3253 — 1545	3267 — 1485	3281 — 1488
3254 — 990	3268 — 1311	3282 — 1419
3255 — 1501	3269 — 1612	3283 — 959
3256 — 1977	3270 — 1021	3284 — 2082
3257 — 1455	3271 — 1694	3285 — 989
3258 — 1484	3272 — 1507	3286 — 1502
3259 — 1247	3273 — 1044	3287 — 1585
3260 — 1128	3274 — 1138	3288 — 1805
3261 — 1554	3275 — 1593	3289 — 2144
3262 — 1069	3276 — 1004	3290 — 1614
3263 — 924	3277 — 922	3291 — 958
3264 — 952	3278 — 1249	
3265 — 1469	3279 — 1392	

4–4–0 '3300' BULLDOG CLASS

3300 — 1556	3366 — 2088	3412 — 1643
3304 — 1029	3367 — 2001	3413 — 1677
3305 — 1569	3368 — 1731	3414 — 2025
3306 — 1071	3369 — 1490	3415 — 1707
3307 — (1694)	3370 — 1943	3416 — 2014
3308 — 1046	3371 — 1047	3417 — 2332
3309 — (1666)	3372 — 1231	3418 — 2026
3313 — 1221	3373 — 1657	3419 — 1471
3314 — (1473)	3374 — 1888	3420 — 1592
3316 — 1609	3375 — 1566	3421 — 1989
3318 — (2227)	3376 — 2165	3422 — 988
3321 — 1258	3377 — 2366	3423 — 1837
3322 — 1627	3378 — 1687	3424 — 937
3323 — 1543	3379 — 1479	3425 — 1062
3324 — 1005	3380 — 1940	3426 — 1519
3325 — 1028	3381 — 1379	3427 — 1857
3327 — 1610	3382 — 1448	3428 — 1919
3328 — (1587)	3383 — 1639	3429 — 1761
3330 — 1689	3384 — 1833	3430 — 1810
3331 — (948)	3385 — 1754	3431 — 2371
3335 — 1040	3386 — 1060	3432 — 1868
3336 — 1665	3387 — 1486	3433 — 1735
3337 — (2084)	3388 — 1555	3434 — 1785
3339 — 1604	3389 — 1493	3435 — 2133
3340 — (1076)	3390 — 1917	3436 — 1525
3341 — 1220	3391 — 1648	3437 — 2152
3342 — 1636	3392 — 955	3438 — 1751
3343 — (1943)	3393 — 2058	3439 — 1250
3344 — (1927)	3394 — 1830	3440 — 1812
3345 — 2139	3395 — 1729	3441 — 1651
3347 — 1918	3396 — 2169	3442 — 1828
3348 — (1730)	3397 — 1465	3443 — 1685
3349 — (1611)	3398 — 2369	3444 — 1767
3350 — 2241	3399 — 1017	3445 — 2045
3353 — 1995	3400 — 2017	3446 — 1638
3354 — 1803	3401 — 1978	3447 — 2135
3355 — (943)	3402 — 1223	3448 — 1849
3356 — 1836	3403 — 1533	3449 — 1745
3357 — (1058)	3404 — 2084	3450 — 2339
3358 — 2102	3405 — 1752	3451 — 1625
3359 — 1764	3406 — 1349	3452 — 2216
3360 — (1597)	3407 — 1615	3453 — 1843
3361 — 1875	3408 — 2212	3454 — 1994
3362 — 1949	3409 — 2227	3455 — 1621
3363 — 1850	3410 — 1829	
3364 — 1618	3411 — 1584	

4–4–0 '3521' CLASS

3557 — (1365)

4–6–0 '4000' STAR CLASS

4001 — (1949)	4021 — 2378	4038 — 1904
4003 — 1696	4022 — 2382	4039 — 1739
4004 — 1776	4023 — 1771	4040 — 2145
4005 — 2316	4024 — 1914	4041 — 1979
4007 — 1706	4025 — 2649	4042 — 1861
4008 — 1710	4026 — 2408	4043 — 2239
4010 — (1767)	4027 — (1831)	4044 — 1933
4012 — 1666	4028 — 2349	4045 — 1790
4013 — 2341	4029 — 1916	4046 — 2379
4014 — 2035	4030 — 2054	4047 — 2325
4015 — 2539	4031 — 1782	4048 — 2648
4017 — 1783	4033 — 2224	4049 — 1844
4018 — 1682	4034 — 2236	4050 — 1644
4019 — 2647	4035 — 1765	4051 — 1674
4020 — 1934	4036 — 2594	4052 — 1853

4053 — 1911	4060 — 1876	4067 — 2136
4054 — 1937	4061 — 1934	4068 — 1713
4055 — 1932	4062 — 2263	4069 — 1773
4056 — 2180	4063 — 1980	4070 — 2650
4057 — 1822	4064 — 2351	4071 — 1777
4058 — 2407	4065 — 1461	4072 — 1787
4059 — 2381	4066 — 1514	

4–6–0 '4073' CASTLE CLASS

111 — 2406	4089 — 2449	5011 — 2588
4000 — 2422	4090 — 2538	5012 — 2448
4009 — 2411	4091 — 2588	5013 — 2605
4016 — 2613	4092 — 2546	5014 — 2606
4032 — 2593	4093 — 2438	5015 — 2621
4037 — 2435	4094 — 2601	5016 — 2608
4073 — 2615	4095 — 2617	5017 — 2426
4074 — 2600	4096 — 2447	5018 — 2534
4075 — 2585	4097 — 2566	5019 — 2611
4076 — 2574	4098 — 2603	5020 — 2612
4077 — 2424	4099 — 2584	5021 — 2396
4078 — 2419	5000 — 2654	5022 — 2565
4079 — 2260	5001 — 2586	5023 — 2637
4080 — 2609	5002 — 2582	5024 — 2638
4081 — 2604	5003 — 2445	5025 — 2639
4082 — 2597	5004 — 2533	5026 — 2412
4083 — 2653	5005 — 2427	5027 — 2640
4084 — 2540	5006 — 2645	5028 — 2641
4085 — 2590	5007 — 2618	5029 — 2614
4086 — 2393	5008 — 2583	5030 — 2643
4087 — 2577	5009 — 2656	5031 — 2644
4088 — 2390	5010 — 2565	5032 — 2564

2–6–0 '4300' CLASS

4300 — 2024	4334 — 1658	4368 — 1984
4301 — 1976	4335 — 1656	4369 — 1747
4302 — 2007	4336 — 1801	4370 — 1664
4303 — 2108	4337 — 1759	4371 — 1635
4304 — 1864	4338 — 2074	4372 — 2376
4305 — 1990	4339 — 1695	4373 — 2099
4306 — 2098	4340 — 2003	4374 — 2052
4307 — 1743	4341 — 2002	4375 — 2053
4308 — 1923	4342 — 2179	4376 — 1999
4309 — 1849	4343 — 2153	4377 — 2207
4310 — 1716	4344 — 2027	4378 — 1760
4311 — 1992	4345 — 1848	4379 — 2036
4312 — 1733	4346 — 1873	4380 — 1988
4313 — 1727	4347 — 1890	4381 — 1931
4314 — 1798	4348 — 1671	4382 — 2154
4315 — 1653	4349 — 1924	4383 — 2072
4316 — 1823	4350 — 2322	4384 — 1985
4317 — 1705	4351 — 1799	4385 — 2175
4318 — 1698	4352 — 1869	4386 — 2131
4319 — 2059	4353 — 1942	4387 — 1678
4320 — 2148	4354 — 1742	4388 — 1987
4321 — 2031	4355 — 1951	4389 — 2103
4322 — 2328	4356 — 1703	4390 — 1804
4323 — 2367	4357 — 1642	4391 — 1736
4324 — 2317	4358 — 2323	4392 — 1762
4325 — 1839	4359 — 2355	4393 — 1968
4326 — 2081	4360 — 2171	4394 — 2354
4327 — 1722	4361 — 2111	4395 — 1784
4328 — 2329	4362 — 1896	4396 — 1818
4329 — 1770	4363 — 2105	4397 — 1634
4330 — 1972	4364 — 1655	4398 — 1889
4331 — 1863	4365 — 2342	4399 — 1986
4332 — 1826	4366 — 2117	5303 — 2172
4333 — 2161	4367 — 1679	5306 — 2155

Tenders being overhauled in 'B' shed.

British Railways

5310 — 2030	6307 — 1971	6347 — 1883	6387 — 2055	8307 — 1723	8366 — 1867
5311 — 1993	6308 — 1748	6348 — 2138	6388 — 1768	8308 —(1999)	8368 — 2159
5312 — 2070	6309 — 1766	6349 — 1661	6389 — 2348	8309 — 2008	8369 — 2010
5316 — 2116	6310 — 1675	6350 — 2063	6390 — 1898	8313 — 2214	8372 — 1967
5317 — 2110	6311 — 2321	6351 — 1746	6391 — 1991	8314 — 1728	8373 — 2326
5319 — 2313	6312 — 1997	6352 — 2156	6392 — 1832	8315 — 1856	8374 — 2324
5321 — 1779	6313 — 2315	6353 — 2350	6393 — 1996	8318 — 1717	8376 — 1808
5323 — 2120	6314 — 2013	6354 — 1891	6394 — 1697	8320 — 2221	8378 — 1632
5324 — 1650	6315 —(1784)	6355 — 1909	6395 —(1723)	8322 — 1633	8379 — 2034
5330 — 2016	6316 — 2331	6356 — 2004	6396 — 1973	8325 — 1794	8381 — 1902
5336 — 2372	6317 — 2076	6357 — 2327	6397 — 2107	8326 — 2073	8382 — 1882
5339 — 1809	6318 — 2112	6358 — 1963	6398 — 2151	8327 — 1753	8383 — 2157
5345 — 2000	6319 — 1669	6359 — 1781	6399 — 1813	8328 — 1719	8384 — 1920
5346 — 2132	6320 — 1672	6360 — 1842	7300 — 1965	8329 — 1637	8386 — 2220
5347 — 1741	6321 — 2333	6361 — 1641	7301 — 1970	8331 — 1964	8387 — 1998
5348 — 1709	6322 — 2022	6362 — 1859	7302 — 2358	8332 — 2338	8388 — 2209
5349 — 2011	6323 — 1670	6363 — 2320	7303 — 1982	8333 — 2203	8389 — 1955
5355 — 1901	6324 — 2375	6364 — 1734	7304 — 1700	8334 — 1806	8390 — 2071
5356 — 1966	6325 — 2121	6365 — 2340	7305 — 2021	8335 — 1738	8391 — 2042
5367 — 1815	6326 — 2356	6366 — 2085	7306 — 2318	8337 — 2377	8393 — 2122
5370 — 1821	6327 — 2123	6367 — 2069	7307 — 1878	8338 — 2146	9300 — 2160
5371 — 1899	6328 — 2149	6368 — 2041	7308 — 2051	8340 — 2373	9301 — 2056
5375 — 2087	6329 — 2068	6369 — 2043	7309 — 2222	8341 — 1841	9302 — 1712
5377 — 2314	6330 — 1711	6370 — 1681	7310 — 1715	8342 — 2361	9303 —(2078)
5380 — 2226	6331 — 1956	6371 — 2009	7311 — 1880	8343 — 2162	9304 — 1929
5385 — 2202	6332 — 2065	6372 — 2334	7312 — 1897	8344 — 2044	9305 — 2219
5392 — 1969	6333 — 2019	6373 — 1676	7313 — 1893	8350 — 1958	9306 — 1744
5394 — 1708	6334 — 2118	6374 — 1946	7314 —(1712)	8351 — 1962	9307 — 2062
5395 — 1732	6335 — 1667	6375 — 2015	7315 — 1910	8352 — 1953	9308 — 2223
5396 — 1660	6336 — 2383	6376 — 2114	7316 — 2086	8353 — 2176	9309 — 2047
5397 — 2089	6337 — 2038	6377 — 1921	7317 — 1724	8354 — 1647	9310 — 2362
5398 — 2113	6338 — 2163	6378 — 2337	7318 — 2077	8357 — 1922	9311 — 2181
5399 — 1683	6339 — 1881	6379 — 1792	7319 — 1737	8358 — 1870	9312 — 2040
6300 — 1957	6340 — 1721	6380 — 2174	7320 — 1954	8359 — 2164	9313 — 2061
6301 — 2129	6341 — 2067	6381 — 2037	7321 — 2125	8360 — 1950	9314 — 1886
6302 — 1845	6342 — 1797	6382 — 2106	8300 — 2029	8361 — 2101	9315 — 2359
6303 — 1699	6343 — 2370	6383 — 1720	8301 — 1811	8362 — 1959	9316 — 1684
6304 — 1961	6344 — 1646	6384 — 1816	8302 — 1927	8363 — 1900	9317 — 1645
6305 — 1749	6345 — 2177	6385 — 1786	8304 — 2345	8364 — 2143	9318 — 2032
6306 — 2346	6346 — 2012	6386 — 1885	8305 —(1727)	8365 — 1981	9319 — 2100

2—8—0 '4700' CLASS

4700	— 2596	4703	— 2532	4706	— 2595
4701	— 2446	4704	— 2571	4707	— 2570
4702	— 2559	4705	— 2439	4708	— 2429

4—6—0 '4900' HALL CLASS

4900	— 2049	4947	— 1539	4994	— 2444
4901	— 2261	4948	— 2256	4995	— 2134
4902	— 2614	4949	— 2258	4996	— (2421)
4903	— 2259	4950	— 2225	4997	— 2530
4904	— 1704	4951	— 1663	4998	— 2598
4905	— 2137	4952	— 2242	4999	— 2616
4906	— 1941	4953	— 1582	5900	— 1852
4907	— 2046	4954	— 2243	5901	— 2567
4908	— 1925	4955	— 2264	5902	— 2602
4909	— 1824	4956	— 2368	5903	— (2634)
4910	— 2230	4957	— 2265	5904	— 2610
4911	— 2229	4958	— 1518	5905	— 2413
4912	— 1960	4959	— 1758	5906	— 2560
4913	— 2563	4960	— 2592	5907	— 2573
4914	— 2268	4961	— 2587	5908	— 2545
4915	— 1560	4962	— 2543	5909	— 2575
4916	— 2210	4963	— 2635	5910	— 2536
4917	— 1947	4964	— 2414	5911	— 2576
4918	— 2246	4965	— 2561	5912	— 2410
4919	— 1871	4966	— 2405	5913	— 2578
4920	— 2127	4967	— 2404	5914	— 2386
4921	— 1714	4968	— 2433	5915	— 2430
4922	— 1913	4969	— 2655	5916	— 2397
4923	— 2245	4970	— 2437	5917	— 2589
4924	— 2249	4971	— 2415	5918	— 2385
4925	— 2247	4972	— 2537	5919	— 2579
4926	— 1952	4973	— 2568	5920	— 2409
4927	— 2250	4974	— 2248	5921	— 2436
4928	— 2380	4975	— 2399	5922	— 2431
4929	— 2253	4976	— 1948	5923	— 2628
4930	— 2251	4977	— 2636	5924	— 2629
4931	— 2374	4978	— 2599	5925	— 2630
4932	— 2141	4979	— 2542	5926	— 2619
4933	— 2432	4980	— 2541	5927	— 2624
4934	— 2252	4981	— 2531	5928	— 2622
4935	— 1884	4982	— 2580	5929	— 2620
4936	— 1725	4983	— 2418	5930	— 2626
4937	— 2267	4984	— 2266	5931	— 1834
4938	— 2232	4985	— 2386	5932	— 2631
4939	— 1874	4986	— 2443	5933	— 2625
4940	— 1825	4987	— 2416	5934	— 2623
4941	— 1775	4988	— 2597	5935	— 2627
4942	— 2254	4989	— 2562	5936	— 2607
4943	— 1459	4990	— 2646	5937	— 2262
4944	— 2173	4991	— 2581	5938	— 2420
4945	— 2234	4992	— 2417	5939	— 2632
4946	— 1915	4993	— 2535	5940	— 2633

4—6—0 '6000' KING CLASS

6000	— 2556	6010	— 2555	6020	— 2403
6001	— 2400	6011	— 2425	6021	— 2552
6002	— 2398	6012	— 2550	6022	— 2554
6003	— 2547	6013	— 2387	6023	— 2553
6004	— 2440	6014	— 2572	6024	— 2549
6005	— 2394	6015	— 2402	6025	— 2395
6006	— 2434	6016	— 2551	6026	— 2548
6007	— 2388	6017	— 2389	6027	— 2442
6008	— 2401	6018	— 2441	6028	— 2557
6009	— 2642	6019	— 2391	6029	— 2392

ACKNOWLEDGEMENTS

The authors would like to acknowledge the assistance of the staff of the Public Record Office at Kew, for making available the documents upon which this book is based. Thanks are also due to those photographers who have come to our assistance in the search for appropriate views of the period, especially W. A. Camwell and W. Potter, to E. Mountford for information on the procedures at Swindon Works, and finally, of course, to Paul Karau and June Judge.

Cover picture: No. 6343 outside Barnstaple shed on 10th June 1935.
                                                        W. A. Camwell

© Wild Swan Publications Ltd. and
Rev. Nigel J. Pocock & Ian Harrison 1987
ISBN 0 906867 34 7

Designed by Paul Karau
Typesetting by Berkshire Publishing Services
Printed by Netherwood Dalton Ltd., Huddersfield

Published by
WILD SWAN PUBLICATIONS LTD
1-3 Hagbourne Road, Didcot, Oxon OX11 8DP